ferment
in the
ministry

ferment
in the
ministry

SEWARD HILTNER

ABINGDON PRESS Nashville and New York

FERMENT IN THE MINISTRY

Copyright © 1969 by Abingdon Press

Standard Book Number: 687-12957-5

Library of Congress Catalog Card Number: 69-18441

SET UP, PRINTED, AND BOUND BY THE
PARTHENON   PRESS,   AT   NASHVILLE,
TENNESSEE, UNITED STATES OF AMERICA

To
Simon
Doniger

Editor, Educator, Social Worker,
Friend of the Ministry

Since 1950 we have worked closely together on *Pastoral Psychology* magazine, he as Editor and I as Pastoral Consultant. I cannot imagine any other nineteen-year relationship on my part that would not have broken the camel's back. Simon Doniger is a great person, and I hereby pay him some small measure of tribute for what he has meant to me and to the general cause of pastoral psychology.

Foreword

Beginning about ten years ago and lasting through the present, we have had a new kind and volume of criticism of the ministry and the situation in which it finds itself today. Even on a second look, none of these books and articles is without validity and merit. It was charged that the ministry had been softened, that ministers were breaking down, that ministers were getting out, that the job description was impossible, that the ministry was a slave of the Establishment, and so on.

These critiques began in the Eisenhower era, and reached their peak in the brief Kennedy period. Under both of these regimes things seemed secure. Pejorative criticism, even if it carried traces of positivisitic Philistinism, could still regard itself as having constructive intent—because, overall, all seemed well. In good times, prophecy about the stench may very well regard itself as constructive.

All this was, however, before our serious involvement in Vietnam, before the race riots in our cities, before the two Kennedy and one King assassinations, and before the incredible fact of the nation's increasing wealth and yet the horrible poverty of many of our citizens had become clear to the public.

This is neither a political nor an economic book, and I have no solutions to suggest for either the nation's wealth or its poverty. But I hope I do have something to say about priests and ministers as we work in this complex situation. We have been going through a period of "failure of nerve," to use the phrase applied originally by Gilbert Murray to Hellenistic civilization. We have become conditioned to listen, Pavlov-fashion, to every conceivable critique of the ministry (and of course of the church as well). Unlike the men who handle jets on our airports, we have had no earplugs that could enable us to separate the sheer noise and push from the genuine problems. Consequently, we have become inclined to listen to the worst we could hear; and, while never taking it wholly, we regard it as a mark of Christian repentance to meditate on the charges as a theological work of merit. Most of us have got on with our jobs of ministry, but with a kind of unexamined uneasiness that does neither God, the church, the world, nor ourselves any good.

For myself, I am through with this well-intentioned but misdirected kind of oblique repentance. Whatever its faults, the ministry in virtually all our churches is more able, better educated, more sensitive to the actual situations of need, and better informed about its tradition, than ever before. It is also, as I shall analyze in the first chapter of this book, in "ferment." But ferment is a stage in the process of wine-making which, while full of agitation and bubbles, comes out at a constructive point if it is not taken as a finality.

I believe I am offering some kind of solution to this failure of nerve in the ministry. My thesis is that the ministry is a unity, a complex unity to be sure, but a unity nevertheless. A complex unity implies some ambiguity, at least temporarily. Therefore, the practical solution to the present failure of nerve comes with a better understanding of the complex unity of the ministry, and capacity to confront the ambiguity of the complexity without losing sight of the unity. I shall argue this thesis during most of the book through cartoon-like images of the actual functions of ministry, attempting to demonstrate that, although details of function differ, they are attitudinally coherent and integrated.

There are new forms and settings of ministry, and new challenges. I trust that my discussion will give them due attention. But to whatever group of general or particular need, and in whatever setting, and no matter who pays the bill, the ministry is finally a general (or "monoepiscopal," to use the scholar's phrase) leadership of any Christian community that is trying to do something significant. New forms of ministry are peculiarly needed in our own day. But if their practitioners have to denigrate all other forms of ministry in order to defend their own, then there is a psychological screw loose somewhere.

This book has been in preparation for almost ten years. In 1958, when I was at the Chicago Theological Seminary and the Federated Theological Faculty of the University of Chicago, the director of the mid-winter conference for ministers twitted me into discussing the ministry today. Thus began the notes from which this discussion evolved. My next excursion into the material was at the summer ministers' conference at Union Theological Seminary in New York in 1960. Then at Brite Divinity School of Texas Christian University in 1961, and at the annual conference of the United Church of Canada on evangelism in 1962. Through these "tryouts" I had only notes.

My first on-paper chapters were for the Cole Lectures at Vanderbilt University in 1964, where four of the chapters were presented in substantially their present form. All the remaining chapters were written in 1967 and 1968, and none of them has been presented in lecture form. I am indebted to my doctoral seminar at Princeton Theological Seminary during the past year for helpful criticisms on the discipline chapter.

In writing a psychological analysis of the contemporary ministry during the past year for the Temporary Commission on Continuing Education of the United Presbyterian Church, which will make its report to the General Assembly in May of 1969, I drew upon the work I had done for this book, but there are no identities of text. In lecturing this past spring at Christian Theological Seminary in Indianapolis, I also drew upon these materials, but also with no identity of text.

My fundamental presentation of a theory of the ministry was made in my book *Preface to Pastoral Theology* (1958). There the theoretical apparatus and reasons for it are obtrusive. In the present volume I am rather more like a pamphleteer. I think the ministry is in much better shape than most of its critics allege. I am trying, although hopefully with some objectivity, to argue this thesis throughout. Hence I have even dispensed with references because I want nothing at all to interfere with my deeply felt conviction that the ministry can make it with a bit of under-

9

standing here and there. As any reader of my previous books knows, I must be worked up to dispense with references.

Because of the piecemeal way in which this book has been put together, I have never had a whole copy I could lend to anybody; hence I cannot thank anyone for reading the whole thing except the readers of the book itself. But I do want to thank, and warmly, the folks at Vanderbilt, Brite, Union, Chicago, Toronto, and Indianapolis for their responses to the aspects of this material that they heard.

I want, finally, to put in a word of appreciation to my Princeton colleague W. J. Beeners, the sole Princeton faculty member who is a better carpenter than I am. When I discovered that, with all its projections into the technological future of civilization, the great IBM Corporation did not make a case that would enable me to take my typewriter to Maine to finish this book, I appealed to Professor Beeners. Between us, we are ahead of IBM; for the typewriter has both gone and returned in perfect safety.

SEWARD HILTNER

Contents

PART I

The Ministry
Situation

1
Ferment in the Ministry

By analogy "ferment" means stir, agitation, unrest, commotion, excitement, or tumult. But the original context from which this metaphor comes, wine-making, includes such characteristics as only intermediate phases of a process whose aim is a stronger product. There is a kairos to wine-making. If fermentation goes on indefinitely, the product is useless. If the proper moment of arrest is seized, however, then the intermediate stirrings and agitations may be seen as necessary stages in the making of a better product.

I believe that "ferment" is a better description of what is happening in the ministry today than are such other terms as "crisis," "maceration," "breakdown," or "upset." Crisis means a point of compelled decision. It implies red and green lights, whereas in fact there is also an amber light that can mean anything from muddling through to new hope. Maceration means softening. It implies a kind of errand-boy failure of nerve, whereas in fact there is probably as much courage in the ministry today as at any time in Christian history. Breakdown means the machinery has failed. It implies that nothing is being done. The fact is, however, that whatever may not be running, it is not the machinery. Upset means being stood on the head. It implies disproportion, misdirection, and even a feeling of tipsiness. In fact, however, most ministers are more puzzled than tipsy. I prefer ferment, with its two clear implications: first, that the stage of agitation may be both necessary and anxiety-inducing; and second, that the result may be very good if the commotion is stopped in time.

The time has come, I think, to move beyond the guerrilla-

15

warfare criticisms of the ministry that have been plentiful in the past ten years. The ferment that they have both expressed and induced may be a very good thing. Such benefits should not be lost. An attempt to return to older certainties will not do. But we should be able to take this particular vintage out of the vats— even if we use a new supply of grapes to start some new fermentation.

The central constructive thesis of this book is that analysis of the functions of ministry (through the idea of images) shows the ministry to be, both psychologically and theologically, a unity— although a complex unity with a variety of types of activity. If the minister grasps this sense of unity within complexity, then he need not feel pulled in sixteen directions. He must still make decisions, hard decisions, about the investment of his time and energy. And he must still be sensitive to the idiosyncrasies in his particular situation. But he will not feel that his job is impossible, or inherently frustrating, or nothing but anxiety. This thesis will be spelled out in many ways throughout the chapters that follow.

The "gimmick" used throughout the discussion is the image, by which is meant a cartoon-like picture that selects central points in the foreground and neglects photographic-like detail that could detract from the needed impression. A large jaw and a cigarette holder could stand, in cartoons, for Franklin D. Roosevelt. A cigar in a determined profile represented Winston Churchill. I believe that, in this cartoon-like sense, the human mind carries out much of its work of perceiving. The trick comes in whether what is selected really is what is most important or not.

The notion of image is not used here in some senses that are, in other contexts, legitimate. It is not used as a mirror-like reflection. Nor is it used as a die-stamp. Nor as a replica. It is not used either as in some modern psychology, as a "self-image," meaning the total view one has of himself. It is used, instead, as an attempt to objectify, with cartoon-like pictures, the inner conception of function, i.e., what one is trying to accomplish. Beginning in Chapter 3, the reader will be carried into the details of my image-clutching.

Since I believe that my complex unity of the ministry thesis, argued out through analysis of images of function, has a chance of getting the wine out of the vats before fermentation has gone on too long, I intend in this volume a message both of hope and challenge for the ministry. That this is a measured conviction, and not hortatory or sentimental wishfulness, I shall try to demonstrate in the present chapter by a brief discussion of the current negative charges against the ministry. None of these charges is without a modicum of truth. But they are all one-sided, and neglectful of the renewal that is going on through the ferment.

Ministers Are Leaving?

The charge is that so many more priests and ministers are leaving the ministry than at any previous time that the ministry must be an impossible vocation. So far, reliable general statistics are not available. But it is probably true that the proportionate number of persons leaving the ministry in recent years is in fact higher than at any time in our century. The actual number, however, is still proportionately small, despite scare stories in the press.

How many of these demittings, however, represent either failure of ministry or failure of man, and how many represent some advance on the part of the persons involved? A few are, perhaps, failures. The majority, I am convinced, are quite otherwise.

I think of two ministers who left the ministry, with whom I have counseled at some length in recent years. Needless to say, my brief accounts of them are designed to conceal all identifying information while also presenting the essence of their respective situations. Minister A was brilliant and had great potential as a theologian. But in a personality sense he was brittle. He was minister of a conservative denomination which had impeded him, throughout his theological studies, from actively relating theology to life and the world. Suddenly he got a new vision about theology, that it was most precisely related to life and the world. He felt released. For the first time, his own faith related to his life. Had he been more of a leader, and less brittle, he might well have returned to his denomination and been a leader in its movement ahead. But some things are irreversible. In a curious way, his leaving the ministry restores his Christian faith personally. I feel certain that God has called him to what he is now doing, which is

17

a kind of secular ministry. He demitted the ministry. But what he is now doing is more for God, and himself, than if he had remained in the ordained ministry.

Minister B was a live-wire social reformer, not exactly hotheaded but certainly precipitate. He was in no sense thrown out of his local church, and indeed continued to be greatly respected by most of his people. But he grew impatient in dealing with the socially conservative minority who objected to his forays into the problems of the world. If he had had more "tension capacity," he would have realized that he could proceed along the lines of his intention, winning some converts and remaining in tension with others, but without jeopardy to his program. Psychologically, however, he was not inwardly strong enough to sustain this tension. Had he continued in the ministry, he might well have broken under it. With his many talents he had no difficulty getting a job with an excellent secular agency; and so far he has done well. Someday he may of course face partial disillusionment in his present work. There are bound to be ups and downs. In a curious sense, despite his single-minded devotion to social reform, his character was too dependent to manage this through the ordained ministry. He needed fewer ambiguities. For the moment at least, he is in such a situation, and I am sure the Lord approves.

Even though Protestants have held, from the Reformation, that every Christian has a "calling" from God, and that ministers are no better in God's eyes than any others, a curious Protestant cloud has looked upon leaving the ordained ministry as something like adultery or divorce. Perhaps it is true that, with some new freedom in this area, some precipitate decisions to leave the ministry or priesthood have been made without adequate exploration of the factors involved. But the freedom itself is good, even if on occasion it may be abused. The new climate requires that the churches, separately or together, provide "vocational counseling" service for ministers of a kind that the past has not known. Some real experiments in this direction are under way, as in my own Presbyterian Church. With some few ministers, we rejoice when they have the guts to leave the ministry. Past ages would have given them no choice, and they would have had to continue in chains to no good of themselves or of the church.

Ministers Are Breaking Down?

There are times when I wish more ministers were breaking down—with heart disease, blood pressure, cancer, psychoses, or criminal impulses. If they did, it might show that they were unhappy victims of commitment to their difficult and complex jobs. The fact is, however, that ministers are the most long-lived of all professional men, and their incidence of serious mental illness is low.

The Board of Pensions of my own church, the United Presbyterian, entered into a relationship with the Menninger Foundation some four or five years ago according to which any minister or his wife or minor children might go to Kansas for a psychiatric evaluation lasting one to two weeks, with most of the bill paid by the Board. No details need be given to the Board; and once the evaluation is completed, the Foundation reports only to the persons involved. Thus privacy is fully respected.

For the period immediately following the initiation of the plan, a number of ministers (together with wives and children) took advantage of the opportunity and were demonstrated to have real mental or emotional problems. In all instances sound counsel was given about steps from that point onward. But after the early rush a new kind of fact came to light. Ministers appeared who, after investigation, proved to be no more mentally ill than other people, but who really hoped that the psychiatrists could call them such—because then the relational problems in the church, or in the family, would not have to be taken as their own responsibility. One could almost say that unconsciously they wanted to be regarded as "sick."

This situation of course points to a relative lack of proper vocational counseling services within the United Presbyterian Church, which we are in process of amending. But from a "breakdown" point of view, the curious fact is that many of these men who were not broken down at all would have, however unconsciously, welcomed a "breakdown" diagnosis.

Since ministers and priests are as human as other people, a certain proportion are bound to have mental and physical ills, in all degrees, regardless of their dedication to their faith and their work. The astonishing fact is how seldom these ills become really serious. When they do, then expert help is needed. Roman Catholics are realistically operating some special treatment programs for priests who become alcoholic or otherwise mentally ill. In the sense of the Presbyterian-Menninger program, Protestants have begun on the same kind of needed and realistic course. Ordination is not a guarantee of continuing mental health. And many excellent persons can be saved by proper programs. Even severe mental illness need not be permanent.

Overall, the "breakdown" theory of the ministry has very few legs to stand on.

The Local Church Is Dead?

Let ministers get into the inner city—in store-front churches, neighborhood gangs, health centers, drug-addict operations, and many other places—and there the church is truly at work. Or let them go into a corner of the globe where there is need, forget the faith temporarily except as a motivator, empathize with the needs of the people, and help the people do whatever is needed to better their condition and obtain more justice. Or let them go, militantly, into any place where they can minister without risk of contamination from existing ecclesiastical structures. We do need ministers in all such spots. What they do may be enormously important. Such sites are the modern equivalent—no matter what the geography—of the foreign missionary movement of the previous century.

The fact is, however, that just like the previous century's overseas missionary movement, none of this is possible if there are not "home churches" to support it. What can we make, then, of those who want to kill the duck that shells out the silver eggs? Why the extreme antipathy, on the part of a few ministers and seminarians, to the "local church"?

I have no new wisdom on this problem, and it is indeed a serious current problem. I am impressed, however, that at my own seminary the best attitude-changer in this regard is actual experience, under competent supervision, in some kind of church

20

situation. It makes no difference whether the theological student is in a local church (and no matter what kind), an inner-city situation, or a hospital. If he is competently supervised, and thus enabled and forced to learn of ministry from reflection on his actual experience, then he becomes positive—although also properly critical—of the ministry of the local church. If, on the other hand, he manages to evade such supervised experience, or has the bad luck to land a situation with poor supervision, then he goes on arraigning the local church.

In connection with our Princeton field education program, we have two suburban local churches where the senior ministers are unusually competent supervisors, owing to both training and natural gifts. Each of them takes a group of three or four students (part-time, of course). The students stick out their respective necks, do what they can in programs assigned to them, and then have the same kind of supervision and feedback that they would have in a clinical pastoral education program. Every one of these students has become enthusiastic about the local church! Part of the reason is surely the competence of the supervision, the selection of graded activities for the students to assume responsibility for, and the acceptance of the students as genuine working subministers. But not a little of it is due also to their being in a group where they can, as peers, exchange all kinds of gripes and praises and critiques among themselves, with or without their minister-supervisor around. They learn leadership through participation. The usual field-work situation of one student provides no such opportunity.

Under the leadership of the late Dean Samuel H. Miller, the Harvard University Divinity School has for some years past invited some minister of a local church to the campus for an intensive couple of days with the students. There have been well-known ministers, and others never heard of by *Time* and *Life*. How many conversions from teaching to the local church have been made I do not know. But the idea and the program are excellent. What is going on in our local churches—with all its obscurity and ambiguity—is the future of the church, for good or for ill. And, in my judgment, not so ill. My guess is, nevertheless,

21

that any of the ministers invited to Harvard have had long thoughts both fore and aft. They could not say no, anymore than one can to the White House. But what kind of weak ethos was Sam Miller getting them to shore up? They must, in fact, have done very well; for to my astonishment I have heard that a few Harvard Divinity graduates have actually gone into local churches.

I know there are local churches that regard their minister as a hired man, others that regard him as a functionary to be dealt with today but happily gone elsewhere next year, and even some that get his political voting record and his children's marks in school before they issue a call. Not all of this caution, incidentally, is bad. Its exercise, since no perfect minister ever shows up, thank God, may lead the church members and leadership into the realization that they too have some responsibility. They cannot ask that the Rev. George do it all. In the interim, however, unless the Rev. George has guts, the fermentation may include some sour apples.

A minority of theological students, when confronted with the complexities of any local church in any site, will want to retreat to something simpler like nuclear physics, where there is some semblance of predictability on the part of neutrons, protons, electrons, and mesons, in contrast to the complexities of both people and church organizations. Supervision may make a decisive difference. Even so, some will find they cannot stand the ambiguity. If so, wonderful that the truth has been discovered so early. The vast majority, however, especially under competent supervision, if they have got this far will go farther.

A minister who cannot tolerate ambiguity cannot tolerate a local church. In many respects, as we now know, the capacity to tolerate ambiguity is a kind of final mark of mental health. One may be low on it and still mentally healthy if the external situation can be arranged to make it unnecessary. But for all complex services and positions, this capacity may make the difference between success and failure. If a minister has very little such capacity, then that is the situation; and the Lord will obviously want him working elsewhere than in a local church. But the capacity, if it exists at all, may be developed. He may "feel ferment," while in actual fact this may be productive adaptation.

22

Laymen Are the Real Ministers?

Through its pronouncements and its collective actions, the church does some affecting of the ills of society. But what is done to this end through church members, in their various slots of social responsibility, is undoubtedly more significant. The responsible J. B. Somebody, who lives in the suburb of Skewed Gardens, a paradise unknown to the poor of Central City, may nevertheless be the chairman of the Improvement Committee of Central City —and mostly because his church has given him some faith and conscience. Maybe the proletariat, Negro or otherwise, will some day skew his gardens in the suburbs. But their chances are much better to get to him and, if necessary, get him to take a more radical line to help them.

Unless I am mostly blind, I see far more responsible and widespread participation of laymen in the churches of the United States than in Europe and the British Commonwealth. Here, our churches have had to support themselves almost from the beginning. The minister has never been able to retreat to a position disclaiming concern for finances. This is in contrast to churches which, at least in the past, were supported by taxation, and where the minister could "forget money." On Stewardship Sunday, of course, this fact can make us look like Madison Avenue if it is badly done. But I think more German churches would have education rooms and kitchens if they had ever had to fend for themselves except during the Hitler regime.

There can be no possible question that the influence of the church upon the ills and evils of the world is carried out through laymen—or not at all. The unhappy aspect about the present ordained breast-beating is that this point is used, surreptitiously, as if it let ordained ministers off the hook about "supervising" what is going on in the impact of the church upon the world. Supervision is not bossing. It is not directing in the sense of giving orders. It is supportive attentiveness, not devoid of criticism, but fundamentally encouraging. Quite literally in heaven's name, why pit ministers against laymen? Why not give each his job description—which was once referred to as his "vocation"?

We have had romantics about the ministry before, and we

have them now. Once we had Baptist farmer-preachers, who preached on Sunday and farmed during the week. Once we had Methodist "itinerants," like Peter Cartwright, who traveled from place to place on horseback and made a point of never settling. If you settled, or made your "living" from ministry, you were suspect. While respecting the motivations of such men, we can see today, nonetheless, the romantic underpinnings of these attitudes. The minister must face the world in all its ambiguity, including his income from the church, and do what he can.

Latterly, both John A. T. Robinson and James A. Pike have been advocating a ministry that earns its living somewhere else and works for the church on its "nonreimbursed time." If some ministers can manage this feat, God bless them. But as a general pattern this seems to me a product of romanticism, taking with insufficient seriousness the "materialism of Christianity," as William Temple called it, and quite likely to produce the wrong kind of guilt feelings in competent young people who are in or who are considering the ministry—as if this activity were not worthy of economic support.

I hope that our local churches will become livelier places than many of them now are, no matter where they are located. Could "The Church" survive without them? By having the courage to close out all local churches that are moribund, unneeded, unduly competitive, and so on, the Church could help to protect the meaning and significance and program of "the local church." But close them out indiscriminately? What nonsense!

No appropriate ministry of the laity can conceivably be in fundamental opposition to the ordained ministry, unless there is a screw loose on either side of the board.

The Church Is the Establishment?

How do we look at the "Establishment" history? Is it the left-wing Thomas Aquinas, Martin Luther, George Fox, Martin Luther King, Jr., Eugene Carson Blake, and others? Or is it the Spanish Inquisition, the anti-Bonhoeffer German Christians, the John Birch Christians, and others? When is the Church part of the Establishment, and when is it a liberal critic going beyond

24

what exists? Every student of church history must give his own verdict. As for mine, with all the reaction that has often been in evidence, I see the basic action of the churches as against reaction and for progress.

The current critique charges the Church and the churches with being part of the Establishment, white, middle-class, tax-free, economically secure, insensitive to the needs of minorities, smug in wealth, sot in structures, bureaucratic in organization. Who, in honesty, could deny a certain amount of truth in all such charges?

At root, however, this charge is not much above the level of the hippies. It implies a first-century romantic bias against the second-century need to find secretaries and treasurers and chairmen—without a St. Paul to appeal to! Specific criticisms of what the denominations are doing, individually or collectively, must always be in order. But the assumption that what they are *always* up to is reaction and holding the line is clearly unwarranted. I am all for specific criticisms of the churches and what they are or are not doing. But global negation of the church as "Establishment"? Nonsense! Nothing can have influence if it has no kind of "establishment" beyond its "first century."

Most seminary students are still in process of winning psychological freedom from their parents or guardians. Talk in the air about the "Establishment" may, depending on the individual student, either provide him with an excuse for not breaking the dependent ties or enable him to find a respectable intermediary object. When I talk with a student, I try to be alert to how much of one and how much of the other is involved. In a way, the same criterion holds for young ordained ministers. If they have *no* criticism of the status quo, probably ecclesiastical rigor mortis has set in. But in that case, I probably do not see them. They come back to Princeton only when they have a problem and a hope. The question, then, is whether their view of their ministerial problem is *open* to what they can do, and they are not mainly interested in getting excused from what they cannot do.

The Establishment—*any* Establishment—is always full of holes. Anybody with a brain and a conscience must be discriminatingly critical of every Establishment. But global rejections—as if the world should have no establishments of any kind? Nonsense!

25

Isolation from the World?

Next Sunday, in the First Church of Nixie, New York, or the Saint Waldemar's Church of Proxie, Alabama, I am sure the respective ministers will declare that love is a wonderful thing, that Jesus agreed with their opinions; so why doesn't everybody get on the bandwagon and love one another—taking it easy, of course, with Negroes, minority groups, homosexual persons, criminals, the mentally ill, and many others? Love them of course, but not too fondly!

How much is the church isolated from the world—both the social problems like race and poverty and the psychological realities like hostility and aggression? The answer to both segments of the question, unhappily, is: Still a good deal—but rapidly decreasing. On the first segment we still have many churches trying to do business as usual, as if they could forget the tough situations and let the government or somebody take care of it. Where this is the attitude, usually the people involved are those who most resent it when the government or somebody does in fact try to do something about it. In my judgment, while these groups and churches are real, they are a minority. The much more frequent situation involves the church that does want to do something about it but does not know how its slender resources can make a legible contribution.

There are two aspects of this church and world business, viewed contemporaneously and functionally. On the one side, it is possible for the church to let the rest of the world go by—and for the minister to concern himself mainly with his pulpit robe equipment, the shape of the baptistry, the architecture of the sanctuary, and perhaps the related facilities such as the educational rooms and the kitchens. All these things are good in themselves if set in proper perspective. On the other side, it is equally possible for the church to become so "worldly" that sermons become trash, worship becomes an outdated rite, and the church becomes so "relevant" as to have nothing to contribute once it gets there.

I still feel profoundly disturbed by the story of the able Lutheran minister in the midwest who fought through, over a year or more, the necessity of his church to involve itself fully in the problems of the Negroes of the community and environs. He did a great job. But when the one kind of victory—compromise —that a Christian can count on was in sight, he resigned. Of this resignation I remain critical. Did he not know that we live in *this* world and not in an ideal world? If he had had no courage, we could wipe him off. But he had! Nevertheless, he apparently had a perfectionism that wanted to deal with the world all at once or not at all.

In this country above all others, whatever the defects of the Church and churches, they are not isolated from the world. Consult your pastor about a problem of marriage or neurosis or delinquency, and hardly any minister will demand that you get it set in "religious" categories before he tries to help you. Since I believe there are always religious and theological dimensions of any such problem, I am not at this point advocating a sterile secularism. But the point is: No conditions—come as you are! When I see some modern miniskirts and slacks, I am tempted to qualify this principle. But so long as decency is preserved, I stand by it. In contrast to my days of youth and vigor, I now have more trouble with the late-middle-aged woman who ought to know better than to wear slacks than I do with the beautiful young thing who fills them admirably. I get along better when I am tempted.

Anyhow, this charge about the isolation of the church from the world cuts both ways. It contains truth in many instances. But the answer to it can never be just caving in, either by retreating into itself or by forgetting its uniqueness.

Should the Church Care—or Fight?

Pastoral care or social action? If the church helps someone to adapt to his situation, is it guilty of depriving him of motivation for standing up against the status quo? If the church, on the other hand, leads him to believe that social action will solve his problems, is it concealing from him the psychological ambiguity he must face in order to live in this ambiguous world?

When should the church care and when should it fight? The one possible general answer is: according to the nature of particular situations. Thus, the harm comes whenever a penchant for one at the expense of the other takes over altogether.

My own professional career began near the start of the modern pastoral care movement. In the early days we were regarded as radical. The seminaries and denominations gave us little attention or help. By the 1960's, however, this movement had won respectability so thoroughly that it is sometimes regarded by the current crop of social action leaders as simply part of the Establishment.

Ever since the beginning of the social gospel movement early in this century, the churches have been seriously engaged in social action. But it seems probable that the pace of this was slowed down for a number of years by some of the so-called neo-orthodox trends in theology. The 1960's have certainly witnessed more fighting activity on the part of churches and ministers.

What I seem now to detect, most noticeably on seminary campuses, is a new, largely unconscious, and rather dangerous notion about what is masculine and virile and worthy in ministry —as against what is held to be feminine, weak, hand-holding, playing into the status quo. The ultimate question I have been asked is, "What do you want us to do, hold old ladies' hands?" And my answer is, of course, "Under some conditions, that is an essential part of the ministry; and besides, old ladies are safer than young ones."

Since the exercise of ministry involves both caring and fighting, according to the situation, the minister who is acutely uncomfortable with either will have a tough time of it. Perhaps each of us tends to lean a bit toward one side or the other; but we can shore up our weak side. The damage comes only when one or the other is renounced.

Theology for Ministry?

It has been charged that finding a viable theology for ministry has become a virtually impossible task. Most pulpit theology, it is held, has never even caught up to neo-orthodoxy, is suspicious alike of John A. T. Robinson's *Honest to God* and Joseph Fletcher's *Situation Ethics*, and simply says a flat No to the recent

28

radical theologies without understanding the problem they are trying, however ineffectively, to solve.

On the other side, the charge is made by many ministers that today's theologians are giving them little help. They tend to write and speak to one another rather than to ministers and church members, it is contended. Even though the issues with which they are dealing are no doubt important, why, it is asked, can they not put their thoughts so as to provide theological help for the minister?

I suspect there is some real truth in both charges. Ever since the frontier began moving westward in this country, there has been a lot of anti-intellectualism in the ministry. And it is clear that in recent years professional theologians (mostly professors) have become far more of a guild than ever before. These are long-term trends that shall require increasing attention and some appropriate correction.

In my judgment, however, it is much more possible for a minister today to find and build a theology for ministry than it has been at any time in my professional career. What has happened is that many of the old taboos or caveats, often unspoken, have either disappeared or been sharply reduced in force. Thus, the minister is freer than he has ever been to build and use a theology that truly makes sense to him. Perhaps the difference is that today he is obligated to work this out himself no matter how many aids he uses. He cannot now merely rely on something given and objective as wholly constituting his theology, as if the Bible or the creeds or the prayer book or Karl Barth or Paul Tillich or Martin Luther were all the theology he needed.

In a way, then, the theological crisis of the ministry is methodological in character. Authorities are still needed; but the authority question is no longer a simple matter of which one. Whatever the authority or authorities looked to, they are insufficient in building a full theology for ministry. One's own part in the task, with all the risks entailed, is now inescapable. This kind of ferment is long overdue. And if we do not move toward iconoclastic radicalism on the one side, or retreat to positive-thinking theology on the other, the interim period will have been worth it.

From Ferment to Function

With the completion of this chapter, and except for side discussions here and there, this book is finished with the prevailing negative charges against the ministry. In speaking to them in such brief compass, I am sure I shall not have answered all the questions of all readers about them. None of the charges, I have tried to suggest, is without foundation. Yet any of them, pushed beyond a certain point, tends to falsify the situation of the ministry today.

I like the metaphor of "fermentation" for the situation of the ministry today. It has been and still is in a stage of agitation. But if we can arrest this particular vat in time, we can get from it an excellent product. The fact that new vats, as always, will soon be needed does not make less important the fact that we had best soon turn this one off.

2
The Nature of the Ministry

This book focuses upon the functions of the ministry as seen through cartoon-like images. It attempts a reasonable degree of comprehensiveness about those functions, but it does not exhaust them. It makes no apology for setting functions in the front row—instead of, for example, the aims of the ministry, the biblical bases of the ministry, the theology of the ministry, the history of the ministry, the structures of the ministry, or many other possible approaches. Good books have been written about the ministry in all these categories, and my discussion is attentive to them. Certainly all these perspectives upon the ministry, and others, are of great importance.

From my experience of leading literally scores of ministers' conferences, however, I have become convinced that most American ministers—scholars though they may be—are functionalists at heart. I do not call us pragmatists (for I belong to this group) only because that term connotes a certain opportunism that I deny. "Functionalist" seems a milder and more descriptive term. We think and feel and work our way into even the most recondite of theoretical matters only by first exploring them in relation to our functions of ministry.

I believe that a similar functionalism is the great strength of American intellectual life in general. In our own field of concern, as in others, a native functionalist approach does not stop with functional analysis. It does move on to basic theoretical issues. And the increasing breadth and originality of American science and scholarship in general demonstrate that a functional be-

31

ginning, among imaginative people, is a motivator for many things, including function, and not a quitting point.

In the sense that my own mind happens to work this way anyhow, beginning with a look at functions, I am a typical American minister. My own explorations into various theoretical realms—including psychology, psychiatry, philosophy, and theology itself—have all been pushed on by my functional beginnings. I can never think something without thinking of doing it. Even the carpentry of the typewriter table upon which these words are being written (the top was made from an old and discarded wooden organ pipe from Miller Chapel of Princeton Seminary) was something I got into in terms of principles only after I had begun some "functions." I believe most American ministers are functionalists, at the start of their inquiries, in the sense I have been describing.

I have, therefore, girded up the loins of my typewriter and decided to breeze ahead—without having a first chapter on the ministry in the Bible, a second on the ministry in the early church, a third on ministry in the Middle Ages—and so on until finally we might get to the present. Of course such studies are of the greatest importance, and I am not ignorant of them. But a functional approach begins at another point and, if it is informed, goes back to the Bible and various stages of history not only for confirmation but also for needed correction. Within the limits of space and knowledge, I believe I have done this in the pages that follow. But if Professor S believes that nothing sensible can be written about the ministry unless the first chapter is called "The Ministry in the Bible," then I shall have to disappoint him. His insights may be even more important than mine. But he got worked up in one way, and I in another. And, if I am not mistaken, most American ministers got worked up through their functions, just as I have.

In every chapter that follows, beginning with the images of preaching, the analysis starts from function; but I trust it never stops there, but leads back to Bible and history and forward to potential creativity. But I do feel an obligation to say first some words from a theological and historical perspective about the minister whose functions are to be examined. That is the excuse of the present chapter. If the reader is already familiar with the current biblical, historical, theological, and new-dimensions discussions of the ministry, let him skip on quickly to the next chapter, where my own creative thinking begins. For those not familiar with many recent studies, however, from perspectives other than my own I present a kind of summary—but it is, of course, from a functional point of view. It asks finally: So what does that say about ministry in the light of what the ordained minister actually does?

I remain respectful of but unintimidated by the notion of the "ministry of the laity." Whatever Christ and the Church need to get done can of course never be done by ordained ministers alone. But neither can any of it be accomplished, especially in our modern world, by some people vaguely known as "laymen" unless the functional leadership activity within the church does something responsible of itself and with the laymen. I suspect that one of the reasons why the Continental churches are now making so much of the "ministry of the laity" is that they have had so little of it. In America we have, happily, had a lot of it. We should, therefore, be able to analyze the ordained ministry and its functions without having to nod every three minutes to Jerusalem or Mecca about the "layman."

The discussion that follows is about the biblical bases and the historical development of the ordained ministry, which means not special privilege but particular responsibility. After that, I shall get on with the central concern of the book—namely, functional analysis, through images, of the functions of the ordained ministry.

History of the Ordained Ministry

Scholars agree that the general structural form of what we now call the "ordained ministry"—according to which a particular person is given general oversight of all the activities of a particular Christian community—did not emerge in the church until early in the second century. This general overseer was at first called a "bishop," which simply means "overseer." The bishop's principal associates at that period were "elders" and "deacons"; so that these three constituted a kind of multiple-staff ministry, but with the bishop as clearly the general coordinator or chairman. There were of course other Christians performing many functions of ministry or service; but they seem not to have held "Offices" in the same sense as bishops, elders, and deacons.

What is known about the ministry during the period of the first century must largely be inferred from the letters of Paul and the Pastoral Epistles. There was probably a good deal of variation in the organization charts. It is clear that ministry at first referred to all the services rendered by the Christian community, regardless of who rendered them. And since becoming a Christian in the first century meant a commitment affecting radically every aspect of life, it seems probable that the actual ministries were complex.

In terms of structure, however, it seems likely that the people who bore various titles in the first century—such as bishop or elder or healer or teacher—were not "officials" holding formal offices, as the bishops, elders, and deacons came to do in the early second century. It is not a correct inference to take Paul's list in I Corinthians 12:28—first apostles, second prophets, third teachers, then workers of miracles, then healers, administrators, speakers in various kinds of tongues—and see all of these as "set-aside" persons performing such functions on a specialist basis. The apostles had a special status as long as they lived, because they had known the Lord personally. Apparently the prophets and teachers did have an informal kind of status. But the other groups, such as the healers, were clearly not "officials."

The first-century picture is further obscured through the fact that Paul does not mention "elders" in relation to ministry; yet other parts of the New Testament show that the elders were prominent in Jerusalem and other places.

The best general inferences that can be made about the first century are as follows. First, the complex and often widely scattered Christian communities were so busy and joyful in performing the necessary functions of ministry that they handled the structural aspects informally, without constitution and bylaws— giving some status depending on the extent of the contribution but not regularizing this. Second, the exception in terms of clearly ascribed status was to the apostles, a point that is of special importance because of Paul's regarding himself as one of the apostles even though he had not known Jesus during his earthly life.

It may certainly be argued from the biblical and first-century data that every Christian, in some appropriate ways, was to exercise ministry, that is, *diakonia.* But there is no evidence that leadership of a proper kind was scorned, or of sheer equalitarianism that failed to appreciate particular talent, even though leadership was not regularized into formal offices.

Many attempts through the history of the church have been made to use the New Testament and the first century as witnesses and prototypes of this or that particular structure of ministry. In the light of modern scholarship, these are bound to fail not only because of the paucity of data but also because the Christians of the first century were not preoccupied with ministry as office. What can properly be permanently inferred about the ministry from what we know of the first century seems as follows.

1. Ministry in general is always the total service of the total Christian community, whether in relation to its own members or to others.

2. Any kind of ministry must, however, be organized, so that leadership is always needed.

3. Leadership should be according to competence, however this be defined. The competence is ultimately functional, i.e., the combination of abilities that can best get the job done.

4. While ministry focuses on communities and their outreach, special respect is to be accorded to the ministry that forms lines of communication among local groups. Witness Paul's own work as chief example.

Beyond points like this, the first century does not tell us what the ordained ministry should be. It has sometimes been argued that the placing of prophecy and teaching in Paul's list immediately after the apostles, with oversight following as a bad seventh, is a structural pattern that should be emulated. The conclusion seems unjustified. The vitality of the community might well rest primarily upon the prophetic witness that curried no favor, and upon the educative processes that cemented understanding of the gospel and commitment to it. But overseer or bishop or administrator ought properly to be interpreted as seeing that those things come first, no matter who performs them. First-century thinking, however, was simply not like that.

From the early part of the second century onward there have been only rare deviations from the notion that a local Christian community should have a general overseer, by whatever name he might be called. This is the principle that we still use in Protestantism about the ordained minister. He is not to perform himself all the functions that are needed. He is not to be a king giving orders without consultation, nor a hired man performing only such functions as the community votes. But he is local "bishop," overseer, supervisor, or facilitator of the total work of the total community.

It is instructive to contrast this almost uniform sociological conception of the ordained ministry in Christianity, Catholicism and Protestantism alike, with the history of the rabbinate in Judaism. Today in Western Europe and America the rabbi is a general leader and overseer just as priest and minister are in Christianity. This has been, however, a recent development. In the long centuries of Jewish life since biblical times the rabbi was the teaching leader but not the general leader; i.e., he was not responsible for overall supervision of affairs. And although there is not time here to deal with the data, I believe a case can be made that Christianity is alone among the religions of the world in this conception of ordained ministry as primarily general oversight over a local religious group, with the consequent obligations about training and competence that call the minister (whether he makes it or not) to some knowledge and skill about all the kinds of functions that will subsequently be discussed in this book. Perhaps it may turn out that the unique structural contribution of Christianity to group life is its implicit conception of "supervision."

During the second and third centuries of the Christian era the office of bishop was taken out of the local community and made into an area or district job. Succeeding the bishop in general oversight of the local group was the priest, the term itself actually deriving from "presbyter," meaning elder. The deacon remained as the principal associate of the priest.

From the third century onward the picture of the ministry was complicated by the rise of monasticism. After the early experiments by individual persons, the group life of special dedication that we know as monasticism began to grow; so that nearly every geographical area had both local churches for people in general and special Christian communities for monks. The abbots became the general overseers of the monastic communities in the same sense that priests were, by this time, general supervisors of general Christian communities. As monasticism grew, it had to have higher supervisory officials over larger areas; and so, under various names, the equivalent of monastic bishops developed. Both power and dignity tended to be ascribed in proportion to territory covered; the larger the area, the greater the status.

As the Middle Ages moved on, the church, including monastic life, became "big business." A group of monks who had entered the order to work (in the field for instance) and pray found that the serfs (tenant farmers) would take care of the fields. Monastic wealth built up, and the monks became entrepreneurs—an early version of secularization of the church. It was against this kind of situation that orders like the Franciscan and Dominican developed at the height of the Middle Ages. They were recalling the church from its newfound privilege of the ministry to *diakonia* and service; and they generally included friars or brothers, since monk or priest had come to connote privilege rather than service.

When the Protestant Reformation appeared, it criticized many things about the priesthood and monasticism as these had developed, but it did not question the monoepiscopal principle; that is, that any Christian community should have a general overseer or supervisor. Attentive to the New Testament conviction that ministry was service, to be exercised by all Christians appropriately, it developed both the doctrine of universal priesthood and that of Christian vocation of all Christians. At the same time it acknowledged "the ministry" as an office, as set apart, requiring preparation and special competence. The office was to be, however, conferred only by the selection of the community—set-apartness, but not imposition. The community to be served had a share in who their general overseer was to be. While the Reformation declared continually that all Christians hold the "keys" in common (not a prerogative of priest or bishop),

37

nevertheless these keys were to be exercised only when authorized by the community. This was a check and balance system. Without an overseer, there would be anarchy. But if the overseer forgot that his exercising of the keys was by the explicit approval of those he served, he would or should be in trouble.

In its conception of ministry, therefore, Protestantism was trying to be realistic about power, yet to recall that all ministry is service. With its strong emphasis on preaching and teaching it paid tribute to functional competence as essential to significant service. And it worked to educate ordained ministers as the church had never worked before. It saw ministry as the exercise of supervisory responsibility but with the emphasis on service rather than privilege—and it saw the content of this mainly in terms of preaching. To separate itself from what it felt was the Roman "privilege" notion, it advised its ordained ministers to wear the *Schaube*, the gown of the secular scholar in the university. But it did, even in dress, acknowledge the speciality of the minister.

When North America was settled, the various churches at first simply carried with them the forms of ministry developed in Europe. But adaptation came very quickly—first to the wilderness, then to the cut-offness from the old countries, and finally to the movement westward of the frontier. Forms of church government differed; but nobody except the Quakers challenged the notion that a religious local community needed a general overseer, no matter whether he lived in (like the Baptist preachers who farmed during the week) or out (like the circuit riders of Methodism).

In America all churches had to begin as new congregations. Hence the function of oversight, of general administration, became crucial in a way it had not been in the state-related churches of the Continent and the British Isles. Changes and alterations were many. But everybody insisted, even while making the most radical changes, that nothing new was being introduced. The functionalism was good. But much of the theory about it was not.

As Christian churches developed in America—and many more kinds of them with the establishment first of religious toleration and then of religious freedom—the ordained minister tended to become more dependent on his relations with his local congregation than was true in Britain or on the Continent. He had to win not only their souls but also their money. If he were not to get fired or become neurotic, he had to develop a political and diplomatic expertise that was unnecessary to his opposite numbers in Europe or Britain. Thus, he had to become more sure of what he was about and of his competence to carry it out; or face more potentialities of disaster. The ministry, too, had its days of "rugged individualism," not in the sense of riding roughshod over other people but in terms of standing up to lonely leadership in a degree that no other group of ministers in Christian history had had to do.

The history of the ministry in America has rightly been called a movement of constancy in the direction of "evangelicalism," at least until the present century. This meant that the church and the ministers serving it were to save souls above all else. It is easy to criticize or even ridicule some of the soul-saving notions and tactics of those days. But the provincialisms should not blind us to the fact that this American evangelicalism was functional in its estimate of the ministry. Not: What is your status? But: How many souls have you saved? Don't tell me your position. Tell me what you have done.

With the emergence of new concern in our own century for the people caught in problems of urbanization, racial discrimination, industrialization, and the like, the churches moved first— through the so-called social gospel movement—to correct the previous emphasis on soul-saving as dealing only with individual persons. In a more articulate way the tasks of ministry came to include work for justice, reconciling beyond the individual's inner self and his family relationships. Perhaps all this at first was a bit too collective, and maybe it believed that progress could be made if you put your mind to it. But it was an essential development.

The social gospel did not talk much about the ministry. But it either exhorted ministers to get to work on social injustice, or encouraged laymen to prod their ministers—so that it accepted fully the fact that the ordained minister was the general overseer of a particular community of Christians.

By the time we reach our own generation, the first major bombshell about the ministry was detonated by Reinhold

Niebuhr. We cannot simply go on with our evangelical concern for the person, he implied, and let other people and other institutions take care of social justice. All efforts for social justice are less than pure or sure, he continued. But the church and the minister must be in on them, even if only 51 percent convinced. The Sermon on the Mount must never be forgotten, but it is an "impossible possibility." Just make sure that our devotion to its ideals does not deter us from getting on with what needs to be done in this contingent world.

After Niebuhr's shattering critique we began to get the impact of the big B's: Barth, Bultmann, and Brunner, and eventually of Tillich. In a loose sense, this movement was called neo-orthodoxy. Its principal instrument was the Bible as understood by modern technical means of scholarship, attempting to be faithful to the biblical message beyond the biblical provincialisms. It tended to emphasize the ministry as proclamation of the Word of God, and sometimes became irrelevantly verbose in the process. Its virtue was the recapture of the biblical message with time-bound elements shorn away; and thus it had a spirit equally compounded of scholarly honesty and theological commitment.

Neo-orthodoxy challenged the pallid commitments to "ideals" and moralistic interpretations of them. It caught the minister up short when he said we should "love one another" and failed to show that love in this sense is an "impossible possibility," or at least very difficult. It told the ministry to stop being so smug about what it had done and to listen to the Word of God about what it might do. It even made a few passes at taking modern science and other knowledge into account.

But neo-orthodoxy, despite its great virtues as corrector, has not been able to achieve a viable reinterpretation of the ministry. It has been shockingly unconcerned about what a minister does— except the ambiguous "proclamation" of the gospel. Eduard Thurneysen has tried to redefine pastoral care as appropriate proclamation of the Word to individual persons and families. All this breaks down. It is an excellent critique that has not found a way of constructing.

In the very recent past, many of the discussions of ministry have been efforts to remind us that ministry is *diakonia*, or service, and relates to all members of the Christian community. This is true and necessary, but such discussion has tended to evade the question: So what, then, is the task of the ordained minister?

As in the long history of the church, we are not today without special interest groups—many of them of merit in what they do—in interpreting the nature of the ministry. Some of them still carry old denominational convictions; for instance, about continuity in the Anglican Church, the rejection of a set-aside ministry in parts of the Society of Friends, the parity of the ministry in the Reformed tradition, and no ordination without a call from a local church as in much of Lutheranism.

The ecumenical movement has stimulated many discussions of ministry that face forthrightly the differences among Christian groups, almost always held by each group to be consequent upon its theory of the church. These differences must still be taken with great seriousness. And yet they are astonishingly little connected with function and service, and are very obviously related to status and privilege. I do not yet know of a serious ecumenical discussion of the ministry that has consistently put function and service in the foreground. Important as they are, discussions of the ministry of the laity, the total people of God, are not substitutes for asking, if the minister is a servant, just what his unique service (and not privilege or status) is to be, and what competence does he have to carry it out. In this book I hope I may be nudging an ecumenical discussion or two to take function seriously, instead of making exhortations about *diakonia* and then discussing ministry in terms of status rather than function.

Some of the special emphases on the ministry today differ, however, from those of the past. Some of these positions flow from concern to minister to people in special situations or settings: the inner city, the hospital, military service, college campus, mission field, and others. It is argued (rightly I believe) that ministry in all such settings requires special knowledge and skills that may not be parts of the traditional preparation for the ministry, and that such education should at least be added to the traditional materials. Up to this point I agree. Some advocates, however, seem to believe that the new kinds of knowledge and skill make the old ones unnecessary. I strongly disagree. In the field I know best,

41

hospital chaplaincy, the best chaplaincy work increasingly performs a wider, and not a narrower, range of the total functions of ministry. I see no reason why this is not relevant to ministry in the other special settings.

Another kind of position about the ministry, which now seems likely to be adopted to a certain extent by the Roman Catholic Church, is to create a group of subministers, who are permitted to perform nearly (but not quite) all the functions of the priest, but who will be trained much more quickly. This might turn out as successfully as has the relation of practical nurses to registered nurses. But the problem is far more difficult, and the parallel far from exact because all nurses work under the general direction of physicians. It is difficult for me to see what functions of professional ministry can be mastered without professional education. Very many functions of the church, under professional supervision, can be done by those not professionally trained. But again, the issue is: ordained ministry, or the office or offices of set-aside ministry.

A third kind of modern position about the ministry (and here there is a variety of views) relates to specialism. The number of persons exercising their ministry through concentration on special functions has greatly increased. In my own church it is now estimated that 20 percent of our ministers are specialists in this sense. Functional specialism may make for much more effective service. But is a functionally specializing minister protected from keeping his mind on anything except the area of his specialty? If he is a Christian educator, does he simply forget that, even for him, preaching and pastoral care are aspects of ministry from which he cannot disidentify himself even if his time spent on them is less than if he were not a functional specialist? Although I am all for functional specialization in the interest of more adequate total ministry, I am entirely against any conception of specialized ministry that tries, thereby, to "protect" people from identification with ministry as a whole. I am even more against those who regard this or that functional specialty as having a special status of its own, whether they be seminary teachers or pastoral counselors.

Also involved in the arguments about specialized ministries

today is how specialized workers in the employ of churches and church organizations, when they are not ordained ministers, shall be related to the churches. In the field of Protestant overseas missions, there are far more nonordained than ordained people. Business managers, social workers, and many others also work for the churches at home. In theory I would hold that, while it is excellent to have such workers, the general oversight should be by an ordained minister—who presumably takes into account all the kinds of needed functions that the Christian community should be performing. In actual fact this may not be good policy in specific instances. Some of the best pioneering contributions of the churches shade some functions and emphasize others. And one expert in the emphasized functions may there be the best general overseer. One of the challenges today is to retain intact the function of general supervision or oversight, in the name and for the sake of the totality of functions of the church, and yet to have some nonhierarchical way of using persons with the needed special knowledge in the work of the church—all over and above the voluntary service of every Christian. The more we can take and understand general oversight as function and not as status, the easier will be the solution to this problem.

In reminding myself as much as my readers of what seem to me principal highlights in the history of the ordained ministry, I have not hesitated to let my position in favor of monoepiscopacy —a general overseer and supervisor in each operative Christian community—be clear. But I have also tried to show that, in Christianity as in no other universal religion (with very minor exceptions), there has rarely been a question about this. There have been thousands of problems. In any local Christian community the minister, no matter what he was called, might interpret oversight as domination, as exuding charm and doing nothing, or in many other irritating or obstructive ways. But only under direst distress have such communities decided to have no overseer at all.

The great historic quarrels about ministry have been, so to speak, geographic. Is the local community its own final authority? Does the overseer of the area have the right to order thus and so of the local community? Or does some kind of representative assembly of a wider area take precedence over any one supervisor or any one community? Today each of these systems of polity (which means political systems) has been qualified, although there are still divisions among them. But there is increasing recognition that whatever their merit—and there may be a bit in each—they are not so much theories of the ministry as theories of ministerial geography. This book is devoted to ministry, not to ministerial geography.

The Ordained Ministry and Functional Competence

Even I, although I have argued throughout this chapter for understanding the ministry basically from a monoepiscopal point of view, have sometimes been nostalgic about the first century, where everybody seemed so keen and enthusiastic (literally filled with God) that things got done and "offices" were not established. But then I get second thoughts about Paul, who, with both his genius and his humility, was nevertheless going to fight all comers who said he was not a true apostle—even though he did not meet the formal apostolic criterion of having known Jesus in his earthly ministry. Had I been in one of those Christian communities back there, I am sure I would have appreciated Paul's visits and his letters to my local group. But I think I would have wondered how he put himself so completely above the political battle. When we reach the postapostolic age, we find, happily, the emergence of the monoepiscopal conception of the ministry, according to which somebody around the place has to keep his eye on whatever is cooking.

There is only one alternative to having a general overseer or supervisor to any kind of local group, church or otherwise, provided there is to be some continuity and performance of functions. That is to have so many codes, rules, regulations, and rituals that everybody involved knows exactly what he is to do—and is of course, therefore, likely to do no more. The Christian church of the early second century lived in this world, and knew that an "organic" body of Christ demanded some kind of organizing.

As all subsequent history, including the Protestant Reformation, shows, however, general overseers are likely to stress their status

44

and power and diminish their functions as service. Even though we are more democratic about it all than previous ages, we are far from immune to the same tendency. Thus, if a minister today is not in process of being ousted, is regarded by at least many of his people as a wonderful Christian, a helpful preacher, a diligent pastor, and so on, he may rest content in this kind of status even though privately he is disturbed at all the kids who drop out of church school, at the inattentiveness of the church to its neighborhood, at the virtual neglect of older people, and at the bourgeois aroma that infects everything. I have met a very few ministers who are relatively unprincipled politicians, but very few indeed. The overwhelming majority fall back into a status not because it has power but rather because they want to be "settled." Today, I think, too many ministers settle for too little power. Some kind of power is needed if service is to be performed. This ought not to be "power over," in the sense of overriding anybody without consulting him seriously. But the retreat to "just doing my job" violates the whole conception of ministry, from the first and the second centuries alike.

With some exceptions, although they are decreasing, the ordained minister today of any Catholic or Protestant church except the fringe groups has had a college or university education, and then an education in a theological school or seminary. Beyond his arts course he has studied an incredible variety of subjects. There is usually both the Greek and Hebrew languages, so he can read the Bible in its original tongues. There is biblical history, theology, archaeology, "criticism," and hermeneutics (what happens to the Bible at the modern end of the sausage grinder). He has studied the history of the Church and churches, and hopefully also a bit about the history of religions other than Judaism and Christianity. He has done systematic theology, historical theology, the philosophy of religion, and maybe even the sociology and the psychology of religion. He has studied preaching, corrected his speech, delved into religious education, and had a go at pastoral care. He has worked on ethics and ecumenics and the "secular society." Maybe—but it is doubtful—he has had some study of how to be an overseer, which is to be the focus of his job from here on no matter what its setting. He has been

45

exhorted to keep on reading, not only "theology" (and what a mixture he has already got) but also novels, history, biography, and every contemporary journal that can get him into the mind of society and the problems of the world.

All this is great; but if his head is spinning—well, why shouldn't it? And nobody knows better than the intelligent minister of today that, whatever he has been able to devour of all this, he has not "mastered" anything, to say nothing of the whole of it.

I admire the modern minister's realism and humility. But mostly I don't like what he does with them. He tends to use them as barricades. In a strange way, and one unjustified by the actual knowledge he has and the skills he rapidly acquires, he tends to become defensive in a professional sense. By running down his own abilities, he unintentionally runs down the ministry. Then along comes some article about "Why I Left the Ministry," or "More Christianity and Fewer Churches," or "The Creative Ministry Without Local Churches," or "Ministers Don't Know Why They Are"—and the poor fellow buckles. Nonsense! No professional man today, even the doctor, has "mastered" his field. Knowledge is expanding too rapidly for that. A great number of ministers are catching on to whatever is valid new knowledge. Some others are throwing in the sponge. But the fact is that nobody can master it all. Perfectionism will not do. The attitude is more important than the achievement.

Happily, continuing education opportunities for ministers are increasing by leaps and bounds, even though far too many of them still are more hortatory and "hand-holding" than they should be. And most of them are too short. In my judgment, a good continuing education course for the minister should begin where the minister has his problems; that is, with an issue of function, of service, of how you do this or that, and then go back to basic principles, wherever you can find them, to shed light on whatever it is. Far too many courses of continuing education insult the minister, even if he does not realize it, by refusing to organize the material in this way. They insist that he take a look at, let us say, Old Testament theology, or pastoral counseling, in their own categories—instead of asking first the functional questions of both Old Testament theology and pastoral counseling.

Perhaps the sessions themselves are good. But if the minister leaves with nothing but a sense of what he does *not* know, then something is wrong. He is not, after all, trying to become a research expert in special theological disciplines. Can he be helped within his knowledge, but utilizing every swotch of it, to use it more effectively in his ministry? That is the question that should be posed to all programs of continuing education. Most of them, in reply, I believe, are not so good. They may do an excellent job on content of this area or that. But when anybody asks "How?" they tend to fade into the distance. Why should not such a program be able, with illustrations, to speak to "How"? Please, brother minister, do not let the august leader off the hook at this point. If he doesn't know how, then he does not know his subject. No formulas. But "hows" are more than formulas. Stand up for your rights.

Conclusion

I have written this chapter under the internal duress of respect for the communicative process. My discussion of the ministry which follows is about the functions of ministry. So far as I can see, in any proper kind of logical sense, functions are what follow from *diakonia*. In my judgment, every minister is at all times sufficiently sensitive to all these functions as appropriate to ministry that, according to the situation, he responds with a dominant emphasis on this function or that. If he has been smart enough to enlist other people to perform many functions of the total *diakonia* within the church and to the world, that is commendable. But he is still, regardless of the setting of his ministry, responsible for appraising what is going on, stimulating more where needed, and encouraging the changing of forms and patterns when the old have outlived their usefulness.

Not only do I believe in the monoepiscopal ministry. I see this conception as also unique, structurally, to Christianity. It has many temptations, all of which have been fallen for in the history of the church. It can become power over, or detachment, or authoritarianism, or busy-work, or much else, in its pathologies. But you cannot have a competent and moving local Christian community without a supervisor, an overseer, who, while dependent upon his community, is nevertheless free at critical points to transcend it. He must be with his organization, but he cannot be merely an organization man.

In the chapters that follow, my implicit argument all the way through is that a lot of the modern arguments about the ministry can be solved if they are approached through the analysis of functions of ministry. No automatic harmony guaranteed. But try it on for size.

PART II

The Functions
of the Ministry

3
The Ministry as Preaching

Ever since the days of the Reformation, the dominant image of the Protestant ministry, often so obtrusive that it threatened to eliminate all others, has been that of the preacher. In cartoon-image terms it has shown a preacher in a pulpit with an open Bible before him.

It will be suggested later on that the total Reformation conception of the ministry was more subtle than this cartoon suggests, and was more complex than it became in some later periods. But it is certainly a fact that this image was primary, both at the time of Luther and Calvin and in most subsequent periods of most Protestant groups.

The preacher in the pulpit with an open Bible before him represented a considerable shift from the image that had been dominant during the Middle Ages. In that era the dominant image, as H. Richard Niebuhr rightly noted, was of a priest before an altar.

Before we come to an exposition of what early Protestants were trying to say positively with their new image, it is important to understand precisely what struck them as negative about the image of the Middle Ages.

The medieval image was rejected for two basic reasons. First, Protestants wanted to reject completely any possible notion that the original sacrifice of Jesus Christ on the cross could or should be repeated in any form in order to make it efficacious for the salvation of men. Whether or not they were right in attributing the motif of efficacy through repetition to the Roman Catholic Church is a question for historians to answer. At any rate, they believed so, and they believed it so strongly that they rejected every image that could carry even a residual flavor of sacrificial repetition. For in the medieval image the priest was not merely praying; he was also offering a sacrifice.

Second, the early Protestants wanted to deny that the priest had a place before God that other Christians could not have. God's saving grace in Jesus Christ was so incomparably great, they believed, that any man trusting solely in it might and should approach its throne. Every trace of the notion that the keys of the Kingdom, or the resources of grace, were held by a particular group of men had to be pushed away. In the medieval image it was the priest alone who belonged before the altar. Hence this image had to go.

The basic reasons for rejecting the dominant medieval image of the ministry were, then, compelling; and, if we leave aside the details, I suspect they still are. And yet there were other meanings symbolized in the medieval image that Protestants did not reject, or at any rate ought not to have rejected. But since the image had to be rejected as a whole, these positive meanings had to go, along with the negative ones; and the loss has not always been in Protestantism's favor.

What were the positive aspects of the medieval image that ought not to have been lost sight of when the image as a whole was rejected? First, there should be no objection to the priest's facing God, especially if he is on his knees, provided only that he is not, in principle, alone. There is everything to commend in the attitude of humility, or thanksgiving, or petition, or intercession before God, so long as the person with the attitude is not usurping prerogatives either of God himself or of the whole congregation of Christians. If the priest, kneeling, had been joined by a nonpriest Christian or two, there should have been no objection to the image.

Second, I believe the early Protestants should have had no objection to priest and people kneeling before some kind of table, provided the table or even "altar" is understood in terms of commemoration and communion and thanksgiving and not as a symbol of pretentious repetition. Indeed, one must go further and say that there is every merit in the reminder that the most extreme sacrifice has been made unto man's salvation. It is not the reality of blood and suffering that is to be eliminated or cleaned up, but any suggestion that the sacrifice by Jesus Christ is not sufficient.

Although this is only a footnote to the main line of this address, we may properly note in passing that some of Protestantism's subsequent difficulties with prayer and the devotional life, and with religious symbolism, come from neglect of those aspects of the medieval image of ministry that ought not to have been set aside.

We can, then, conceive the possibility that early Protestants, instead of creating a wholly new dominant image of ministry, might have corrected and cleaned up the medieval image. The priest could have been joined, in the revised image, by other Christians. The altar could have become a table or a praying station. Perhaps a cross, if rude enough, could have symbolized the once-for-all character of the sacrifice being recalled. But the fact is that the Reformers, who felt they were confronted with a revolutionary, all-or-nothing situation, were in no mood to tinker and amend. They had much bigger apologetic fish to fry, and for their purpose an entirely new dominant image was needed.

The Intent of the Preaching Image

The new image was a preacher before a pulpit with an open Bible. The positive intent of this preaching image was as follows.

First, the presence of the Bible showed the centrality of the Word of God. This was not, as we shall see on further analysis of the image, a naïve biblicism that equated God's Word with the literal words of the Bible. But it did rightly declare that the Word of God comes to men through the Bible, and hence the Bible is indispensably present in the image. If men are to be at all attentive to the Word, they must do so through attentiveness to the Bible, not necessarily exclusively but always normatively. The Bible is both the primary communication medium and the criterion of truth.

But the image, second, is not confined to the portrayal of the Bible. There is present also a human being, a preacher. To human beings the Bible is not automatically self-interpreting.

53

Whatever the Word may be, it is not an automatic answer that comes through the Bible as the solution of a complex problem in mathematics today comes through a giant electronic computer. The Word requires human communication. The Bible, giving testimony to the Word, requires human interpretation. Thus the preacher in the Reformation image was not excess baggage. He was not a concession. He was not present simply to symbolize human beings as receivers of the Word, although he was indeed also a receiver. He and his function are declared, by the image, to be necessary to the proclamation, communication, reception, and assimilation of the Word. It is clearly out of order to make apologetic statements about the presence of a preacher in this image. He is just as important to the whole intent of the image as is the Bible, and this fact should be stated authoritatively.

Third, the image also contains, in addition to the Bible and the preacher, a pulpit. In modern language the intent of the pulpit is to symbolize connectives or connectors. The pulpit is a connector in two senses. On the one hand, it is the means of relating the preacher and the Bible; and, on the other hand, it is a means of relating the Word from the Bible through the preacher to the people, including the preacher as, along with the people, also a receiver. Thus the pulpit is not simply a symbol of any old kind of connection, but of a connection that is proper and patterned. If we had a Bible and a preacher but no pulpit, the kind of connectedness that might exist between preacher and Bible, and hence between people and Word, might be quite arbitrary. Or, to use modern language, it might be professionally irresponsible. The pulpit symbolizes responsibility to the people. Even the truest of words, to put it sharply, are not enough if they contain no responsible attempt at communication. Thus the pulpit too belongs in the image. It is as indispensable as the Bible and the preacher. The total image conveys the many and subtle relationships among this triad: Bible, preacher, and pulpit. Without exhausting the image, at least a few additional aspects of the subtle symbolism of the image may profitably be mentioned.

There is, for example, the fact that the Bible is open. We may hope that it was not opened for the first time only when the preacher approached the pulpit. Certainly, as early Protestantism made clear, it had to be studied, as diligently and intelligently as possible, well in advance of any specific attempts to preach. And yet such study, the image tells us, was never to be rounded off in such fashion that the preacher could dispense with the open message during his preaching. The Living Word is a contemporaneous Word. It is not enough even for the preacher to have been attentive to it an hour, or fifteen minutes, before preaching. Even a recently warmed-over Word is still a leftover; and no matter if it were once cooked with gas or even radiant heat, it is still unfit for human consumption if the covers are closed around it now.

The fact that the Bible is open during the preaching says something to the people. It says that the preacher is contemporaneously, right now, attentive to the Word as it works right now, and not merely to recollections, intimations, memories, impressions, or other historical data. It suggests that every point he makes is, right now, checked against the message of the Word conveyed through the Bible.

But the Bible's being open has also a symbolic message to the preacher. The coincidence of open Bible and open mouth comes in that order, and not in reverse! Revelation precedes otolaryngological demonstration. Geographically speaking, his preaching is always over and through the Bible, since it is open. It is never merely about or across the Bible. If the Word does not, right now as well as in previous study, speak to him, it cannot speak through him to the people. But let him have no feelings of deprecation about manifesting his tonsils. The open mouth is necessary, proper, and good, regardless of its dental aesthetics. Even smelly molars or tonsils laden with staphylococci, while not recommended, cannot impede communication of the Word in preaching. If the Bible is truly open, the mouth may also be open—without apology.

Another subtlety of the image is about who holds what. The Bible is held by the pulpit, not by the preacher. And that which holds the pulpit, whether it be floor, dais, or chancel, also holds the preacher. The preacher has no standing not shared by the pulpit. And the Bible is so supported that the preacher need not worry about its falling. Both preacher and pulpit have a common foundation.

The symbolism of all this is virtually self-explanatory. The pulpit, which represents both the people and the preacher's professional responsibility, not only shares its foundation with the preacher but is also on the same level as he. The people are not inferior. The preacher is no better than they. He stands where he stands, which is an uplifted position, because of his functional responsibility, not because of his character or his merit. It is not he who is lifted up but his function; but since he is lifted no higher than the pulpit, so are the people lifted up in their function of hearing and receiving the Word. Whatever lifting there be is shared.

Yet another suggestion of the total image concerns the way in which living and non-living realities are to be joined in human life and for human salvation. The Word is a living Word, but it is testified to and conveyed through a Book which, as book, is not organically alive. The preacher is a living human organism, as are the other people to whom the Word is also life and salvation. Preacher—Word—people: these are all alive. Discourse—Book—behavior: these are all, in a significant sense, dead because they are nonorganic. But life, the image suggests to us, is never to be apprehended with simple directness, alone and in itself. The order of the Word is "no angel visitants, no opening skies." It is, instead, through death to life, through the nonorganic to the organic, through the Book to the Living Word, through the three dead homiletical points to just possibly a receptive heart or two. Homiletically speaking, in the midst of life we are in death; and only if we learn to tolerate death—a Book and not an angel, an idea and not just a feeling, a conviction and not merely a charitable impulse—can we approach life.

The Reformation and Medieval Images

Having now set forth at least the principal meanings and symbolic implications of the dominant Reformation image of the ministry, we may return to a comparison and contrast of this image with that of the medieval period: preacher–pulpit–open-Bible in relation to priest-before-altar.

We are at once constrained to ask of the Reformation image: What has happened to knees? Are we not to confront God, or is it enough to confront one another? And why are no people but the preacher shown? Let us consider these questions in order.

We begin with knees, housemaid's or otherwise. Can the dominant Reformation image of the ministry be tenable if nobody is on his knees? Can even God tolerate a people and a preacher who have presumably taken his work in the sacrificial and costly atonement of Jesus Christ, his Son and our Lord, if their leading image of ministry and servanthood is devoid of genuflection? Is it "stiff-necked" to substitute stand-up talk and sit-down listening for the thanksgiving and confession that call for some other posture? Perhaps the priest in the medieval image had an inflated notion of the power of his knees. But at least he acknowledged, by his kneeling, God's transcendence. In the preaching image, who acknowledges any transcendence to anything? The preacher is looking horizontally, alternating between a dip at the open Bible and a stance toward the people. But in neither instance is he truly bowing his head or raising it in adoration.

In the Reformation image there is a book instead of an altar. An altar at least implies sacrifice, once-for-all or otherwise. But a book—paperback, hard-cover, first edition, or translation—may mean almost anything, or nothing. How can a book, even the Book, substitute for the clear and concrete symbolism of sacrifice on the part of our Lord Jesus Christ, Son of God, who became flesh and suffered on the cross for our sake? Surely a book is poor even as a reminder of what, through sacrificial atonement, has given us life. And the preacher in the Reformation image, whose sides have not been riven, is hardly a compensation.

The only sustainable answer to these objections is that the Reformation, while frying its particular fish, expected the toaster and the coffee pot and the sandwich broiler to be going on as usual. It was not against kneeling or atonement or prayer, or looking upward to God. It thought that it took such things for granted. But their absence from the explicit image of ministry is

57

not above reproach, and we may continue to ask about knees and transcendence.

When something is taken for granted and not articulated, it may cease to serve as a check on various possible kinds of distortions. Thus the absence from the dominant image of the ministry in Protestantism of the permanent truths in the medieval image helped later Protestant rationalism and intellectualism to become stiff-necked and rigid and even arrogant; pietism to become detached and legalistic and self-righteous; emotional and anti-intellectual groups to become aesthetically barren and theologically illiterate; and some liturgical-minded groups to conclude that the calluses on their knees entitled them to wear plugs in their ears.

There is certainly nothing in the Reformation image itself that gives warrant for rigidity, legalism, obscurantism, or wooliness. The fact that the preacher is standing before the open Bible and pulpit is not a negation of prayer and adoration but is making central the communication and reception of the Word of God. The fact that the Bible is open on the pulpit is no denial that forehanded Bible study is needed. The presence of the pulpit in an elevated position is no invitation to arrogance or dogmatism, but a symbol that both preacher and people are lifted up to hear the Word of God. And the fact that a human being is a necessary communicator of the Word surely does not make his communications infallible.

Yet it is unmistakably true that some of the distortions of the preaching image have resulted, directly or indirectly, from the loss of positive elements of the medieval image which were discarded, along with the unacceptable elements, when the new Protestant image was created.

Pathologies of the Reformation Image

The most serious, troublesome, and subversive distortions of the ministry in Protestantism have come, however, from literalizing some single aspect of the preaching image and ignoring the indispensability of all the parts and the subtlety of their symbolic interrelationships.

Some of the pathologies of the ministry have already been alluded to, but we shall now try to be more systematic. First and most obviously, there is distortion when any one of the three main elements in the preaching image is lifted out of its context and set forth uncritically. If this is done to the Bible, even to the open Bible, it leads to biblicism or fundamentalism. The Book is confused with the Word. The preacher becomes a cross between a detective and a district attorney. And the pulpit becomes nothing but a reading stand. Surely this is pathology.

An exclusive emphasis on pulpit is also a distortion. This may mean such an exaltation of worship or of church edifice as the setting for preaching that the missionary nature of the church is forgotten and the Word is brought only to the supposedly faithful. Even more disastrously, it may mean that the central function of ministry is felt to be a discourse on Sunday morning, containing a lead, three points, and a thought for next week, not to exceed twenty-five minutes in length, set forth in a tone any self-respecting human being would reject if approached privately. Again, wrenching pulpit out of context may make it into a kind of barricade, so that utterances from behind it are impenetrable to criticism except by God, who has, with this kind of performance, undoubtedly slept through the whole thing and is too bored to criticize.

When the preacher is taken out of the context of the preaching image and treated as the whole ministerial cheese, the results are the most dire of all. This may lead to preacher cults, which are not ordinarily started by ministers but are too often gratefully received by them. A preacher who is very short on theological acumen, biblical understanding, existential relevance, and human sensitivity may nevertheless receive adulation if he has something that will probably be called "personality." Without advocating drabness or monotony, and certainly not the denial of the minister's individuality, we may properly look askance when both Bible and pulpit receive only conventional nods and neither is permitted to stand in the way of the preacher's rapport with his audience. And it is, in this instance, an audience, and neither a congregation nor the people of God.

It has always interested me that the principal point made in the account of the first group of run-of-the-mine Christian preachers, the seventy, is aimed precisely against this distortion in the outlook of the preacher. When the seventy returned from their first engagements, they reported, in astonishment and delight, that the tools and powers given them by their Lord in his commission had actually worked. They were told by Jesus, "Do not rejoice . . . that the spirits are subject to you; but rejoice that your names are written in heaven."

To take any one of the basic elements of the preaching image of the ministry, therefore, as exclusive, or to lift it out of context of the whole, produces pathology; and hardly anything that can be imagined has failed to happen in actual life. But there have been other distortions of the ministry when the delicate relationships among the elements of this image have been lost sight of. We shall note a few of them.

One such distortion is a kind of premature closure on this image as if it represented the whole goal of Christian faith and life instead of what it actually is, the basic mode of ministry to evoke faith and life. One of the real glories of the preaching image is its unabashed concern with means as essential to the achievement of ends. It shows its faith that the goals will come if there is faithful attentiveness to the communication of the Word. Its suspiciousness of goals, inattentive to the means of approaching them, is thoroughly dynamic, entirely correct, and certainly biblical.

But the preaching image of ministry is not the goal of either Christian faith or Christian life. One distortion, of which such a sophisticated theology as Barth's is not entirely innocent, is so to cloud the distinction between the preaching image and the faith and life of the people, including the preacher in the world, that speaking and hearing a reasonable facsimile of the Word of God is in danger of being confused with the mission of the church to the world and the vocation of Christians before God but to the world's need. If you want more cartoon images, as my mind always does, think of this particular pathology as the "hydraulic fallacy." The Living Water of the Word, by this analogy, gushes down from heaven by spiritual gravity and divine love, and pulpits are or ought to be its fire hydrants. So far, the analogy has much to commend it. I also like the general suggestion that the congregation can do with a drenching, provided it is conceded that all properly human hydrants have a leaky valve at the rear, to assure that the preacher also gets wet. But from here on, hydraulics is deceptive. People and preacher will get dried off, at least until next Sunday; and the water runs down drains or ruins carpets, doing no one any good in particular.

I do not quite know how to save this figure of spiritual hydrology for the Kingdom of God without a bit of silliness. But if you will stand that, it can be done. Suppose that both preacher and layman are equipped with living water sacs. Today, of course, these would be leak-proof, flame-proof, loss-proof, and thermally insulated. Each sac will be no bigger than the person can handle. But each sac will also have a good spiritual sprayer attached, wholly free of technical complications. As we might say today, fully dynamic but with no moving parts—which is nice work if you can get it. Anyhow, each sac, in our imaginative picture, is used to spray living water during the next week precisely where it has the greatest chance to do good. Thus, the real box score of the act of ministry symbolized by the preaching image is not back there at all, but is rather in the appraisal of the remote and mundane hydrolosis the next week. To be sure, I agree that all this carries hydraulics a bit too far. But I am a bit tired of contemplating those drenched parishioners back in their pews. If they are stupid enough to sit there until they get pneumonia, let them not blame it on the Word. No doubt they will be prudent enough to dry themselves. But the fact is that the living water is not just for them; it is for their ministry to the world. If we really want to perpetuate this hydraulic analogy, we must go all the way with it; and I have the appalling fear that the end product may be a new kind of hosanna!

Less popular than the hydraulic notion of ministry but even more reprehensible, if you will continue to permit these analogies from elementary physics, is what may be called the "gaseous image of ministry." According to this, and no doubt in the name of something misrepresented as Spirit, everything becomes vaporous. The Reformation image, with a heavy Bible, a weighty pulpit, and an overweight preacher, all fades into some kind of aura. The gaseous goal of ministry is the creation of some kind of subjective feeling. Commonly this feeling may be described as good, as comfortable, as relieved, as positive, or even, so help us, as Christian. But it may be more subtle. It may be a feeling of "Thank God he beat me to a pulp" when the preacher has let loose with some version of fire and brimstone, even the cellophane-wrapped kind of our day. In any event, the gaseous figure of ministry limits its conceptions of the functions of ministry to subjective feelings as experienced here and now. I find myself too gravely tempted to comment, and cannot resist, that the individual molecules of a gas are wholly unpredictable and that we can predict only their mass behavior. Thus the gaseous figure of ministry is, despite its disclaimers, inherently impersonal and anti-individual. The true preaching image of ministry is not.

I have dealt with liquids and gases, and you may well wonder if I have anything to say about solids. Of course I do, but it is a bit anticlimactic. In the Reformation preaching image the Word of God may wrongly be equated with the solid lines of type in the book; the solidity of the pulpit may be misrepresented as the authoritativeness of something or other; and the preacher's power to interpret may be mistakenly equated with some kind of weight —not necessarily the girth of his stomach, but perhaps the athletic cut of his shoulders, or more probably the weightiness of his voice. You may, if you like, pursue the figure of solids, and profitably. But these implications are, if I may say so, "duck soup." Liquids and gases, on the other hand, are elusive, and deserve the greater attention they have been given.

Let me remind you that the immediate point has been pathologies in the conception of ministry arising from subtle distortion of the relations among the three elements in the dominant Reformation image of ministry: Bible, pulpit, and preacher. I have turned to the most elementary notions of physics to get at some of these. With equal profit I might have turned to elementary chemistry and shown, for example, that our useful and harmless table salt comes from two deadly poisons, sodium and chlorine. To be sure, in that case I might have to put on an argument to demonstrate that the Bible and the preacher are both deadly poisons—but I think that I finally could manage this.

In this brief account of pathologies of the preaching image I might of course have gone lightly on figures and analogies and moved heavily toward literal description. Since the Bible does not change, and the pulpit changes only aesthetically, that would have meant describing one or another kind of distorted attitude in preachers. Preacher attitudes may be narcissistic, solipsistic, arrogant, aggressive, masochistic, dependent, detached, wistful, whimsical, smug, snobbish, threatened, and so on to the limits of the dictionary of pejoratives. But is there any real value in a systematic categorization of all the attitudinal ills that preacher flesh is heir to? Perhaps there might be. Certainly all preacher flesh including my own, needs to think in self-appraisal about such matters. But the elaboration of this notion is not my task at this point, however important it may eventually be to our common concern.

For now, it is enough to acknowledge that the very best image of the ministry, which might or might not be Bible-pulpit-preacher, is always subject to pathological distortions. If it were not so, somebody like John Calvin would have assured us. Since he did not, we must make the best of it, and resolve to analyze the pathologies.

Preaching and . . .

I have indeed attempted to interpret and defend the basic Reformation image of the ministry, with its representation of preacher before open Bible on pulpit. There is nothing in any age —be it atomic, anxious, organization-man, or one-world—that renders this image superfluous, if we understand it aright. No apologies are needed for its projection into 1975.

What this image properly declares is that the Living Word of God is relevant and decisive for all sorts and conditions of men provided they will hear and heed; that the Word comes through men who, even until the eleventh preaching hour, study and try to be receptive to it as given through the Bible in dialogic reflection upon life experience; and that the pulpit is the juncture point of Word and interpretation. This image is basic but not exhaustive. It assumes things that are not made explicit in it.

Backward, it assumes a Christian community that comes to church not solely to feel better but also to find its Christian duty and vocation. Forward, it assumes empowerment and guidance on what the Christian—every Christian—actually does in and to and for the world.

No single image can get all that in. Every image must be a cross-section. It is like a color slide. Perhaps this is why, with all my concern for movement and dynamics, I have finally given up home movies and have concentrated on stills. Properly presented and interpreted, stills also may be dynamic, as the preaching image shows.

Like every other image of ministry that will come before us for serious inspection, the preaching image emphasizes some things and neglects others. Always, in order to understand properly the emphasis a cartoon image is making, it is necessary mentally to add to it what it assumes but does not make explicit. In the preaching image we need especially to add the following items. First, a congregation is to be added. It is now presupposed. Second, add a previous view of the preacher working on the open Bible in his study before he comes to preach from it in the pulpit. Third, add a later view of preacher and congregation all going out into the world, to serve its needs and to communicate the Christian gospel to it. Fourth, add some befores and afters that include prayer, adoration, singing, and communion. The preaching image is properly set in this larger context, and we distort it if we are unaware of that context. But of course if we insisted on the literal inclusion of all these elements, we should have no image at all but only a kind of filmstrip. Let us, by all means, keep the image. But let us be aware of why it emphasizes what it does.

Preaching and Pastoral Care

The continuing utility of any particular image of ministry depends partly upon what we find, on analyzing it, that it truly represents, and how important we believe that to be. But it may depend also upon our ability to separate from the image some kinds of meanings that may have become attached to it and which conflict with meanings of other important images that we wish to retain. In our day one of the most important questions about the preaching image is this: Does it conflict with pastoral care? Even though our account has not yet set forth the image of pastoral care, we can still make a preliminary appraisal of the preaching image to see whether, as is often charged, it is in opposition to the ministry of pastoral care.

The question is sometimes posed in this way. In preaching the minister is supposed to speak from the Word of God, and he is not to please or placate any man. He is to speak the truth in love as God gives him to see the truth. But in pastoral care we are told to listen to people, to accept them, to be sensitive and considerate, to see things from their point of view. Can these injunctions be reconciled? Or must a minister be one kind of person in preaching and quite another in pastoral care?

We may begin to get toward an answer to this question—and I believe there is one—by first making a longer statement of the question from each perspective.

In preaching the minister must indeed speak the whole gospel—not in every sermon, but eventually. Indeed, each partial speaking should point beyond itself in the direction of the whole gospel. And the minister should speak with humble authority; that is, with an authority that transcends his person but is humble in its awareness of the limitations of that person. He humbly acknowledges himself to be a kind of midwife, and yet he knows he is charged to perform that function creatively. He cannot simply tell a congregation what it may want to hear, whether that is a coddling or a spanking. He must do his best to let the gospel speak truly, let the chips fall where they may. Even when he speaks "comfortable words" as appropriate parts of the gospel, he must remember that such words are to "enhearten" and not to make easy.

In pastoral care it is certainly necessary, whatever the minister may try to do eventually, that he begin by getting as far inside the frame of reference of the person as the person permits him to do. Not only is this necessary for any understanding of the other person in his concreteness. It is also necessary if the pastor wants to convey to the person acceptance that undercuts conflicts and divisions and doubts and fears. Acceptance is required not only at the horizontal level of interpersonal relationships but also in order to convey, beneath all the difficulties, the acceptance by God himself. If the pastor rejects part of the person, then it is difficult to demonstrate what God's total acceptance may mean. And thus in pastoral care we do attempt to listen, to understand, to accept, and to clarify. We do not sound off lightly, telling the person what we think he should do with no notion of how, from the inside, he looks at life.

Are these two approaches as restated, then, incompatible? Do they require two different kinds of minister? Or is the apparent difference between them only situational and not fundamental? I believe the last to be true.

The preacher is indeed to preach the whole gospel. But as our image analysis has shown, he preaches nothing to other people that he does not also preach to himself. If that is so, he cannot possibly, on psychological grounds, treat the gospel as if some aspects of it merely called down vengeance on people. He can preach the critical, wrathful, or law aspects of the gospel to himself as well as to other people only if these judgmental dimensions are understood in a context of love that transcends or undercuts them. So understood, they may at times be negative, sharp, or hurting, but never simply so, and never out of context with a deeper love that makes the hurt or the sharpness both tolerable and acceptable.

Only the man who knows he has been forgiven can know the enormity of his sin. Only the preacher deeply aware that even God's judgment is a manifestation of his love can acknowledge its reality, for himself and others, and realize that the very capacity to acknowledge it is itself a demonstration of the grace that guides it. And since he is communicating this subtle relationship to others as well as articulating it for himself, he cannot possibly succeed unless he gets inside the frame of reference of others. If they view God's judgment as a simple negativity, and react defensively against it, he must acknowledge and articulate this error, and demonstrate that it is an error. Even his most prophetic utterances cannot remain unconcerned with the frame of reference of others. He may indeed try to alter opinions, to correct errors, to demonstrate truth. And some people may reject his interpretations. But a God whose judgment is only a situational difference within the context of his love cannot properly be represented, at any point, as intending a simple negative.

When we turn, in the light of these preaching comments, to pastoral care, the critical question is whether the attempts to understand and accept, to get inside the other person's frame of reference, to apprehend and help to clarify the nature of his specific conflicting feelings, all together imply the absence of judgment. The answer is certainly not; instead, this is the one framework in which judgments in the Christian sense can be realized and accepted.

Suppose that you or I, in exercising our pastoral care function, have done all the things that my books on this matter have advocated and which I sometimes remember to carry out myself. Suppose that we have been understanding; that, without probing or pressing, we have grasped the subtle and specific nature of the interior and conflicted viewpoint of the person, and have begun to help him sort out and clarify all these inner feelings. Certainly the person, with this kind of help, will begin to feel some kind of release. But release is never unaccompanied by exposure. The joyful awareness that some shackles have been removed is at once followed by the recognition that the old defenses and excuses, previously justified by the shackles, will no longer do. One is tempted, despite his new joy in freedom, to revert, to deny that the more realistic self-judgment is meaningful and relevant. The critical and decisive stage comes when he either accepts the new judgment as benevolent or retreats from it. He simply cannot enjoy the gains of freedom without accepting the responsibilities it brings. With pastoral help, he may take both.

Thus, the true manifestation of acceptance and understanding in the relationship of pastoral care is not some simple positivity, as if one felt two degrees better today and four degrees tomorrow. There is no simple upward line. If genuine, learning to feel joy means, should the situation warrant it, equal increase in ability to feel sad. In pastoral care all this has little or nothing to do with who says what to whom. The experience of assimilating judgment is impressively important. The pastoral utterance of judgmental words may or may not be relevant to this end, and certainly is not relevant if the context appears to be rejection or misunderstanding.

Preaching is not, procedurally speaking, pastoral care to larger numbers of people. Pastoral care is not, procedurally speaking, effective preaching to one person. Such literalistic notions distort both functions. But in terms of fundamental aims and attitudes there is astonishingly little difference between preaching and pastoral care or pastoral counseling. Both make progress as that which is unpleasant but necessary becomes capable of assimilation because of the context, environment, atmosphere, and conviction that manifests the love within judgment, the grace within or beneath law, the freedom within responsibility. And in preaching and pastoral care alike, apparently these things can appear only in relationship.

There are many procedural differences between preaching and pastoral care. Both involve realms of expert knowledge that must be studied directly and cannot merely be inferred or derived. But if these learning processes have been undergone, through experience as well as thinking, then it is unthinkable that preaching and pastoral care, rightly understood and humbly practiced, can be in fundamental contradiction within the functions of the Christian minister.

4
The Ministry as Administering

In the current ministerial vocabulary, administration is a dirty word. When ministers get together after hours at a convention, the complaints that are not about money and bishops are nearly all about committees, women's societies, the telephone, the mimeograph, denominational programs, correspondence, and various related matters all generally classed as "administration."

This commonsense impression received significant reinforcement from the study made by Samuel Blizzard, the full report of which is still unpublished. Roughly speaking, when Blizzard's five thousand ministers were asked what aspects of their duties were most and least rewarding, they declared preaching and pastoral care to be most rewarding and administrative and executive functions to be least rewarding. But when asked about their actual time schedules, they reported spending more time on the latter than on the former.

So convinced am I of this general ministerial dislike of admintration that I believe I know exactly how this discussion could achieve, for me, a peak of popularity. I could begin with tears over the mimeograph and the telephone, make resounding remarks about the minister's need for plenty of time to study, portray the number of dying persons deprived of pastoral service by committee meetings, and declare warmly that the Word and sacraments should not be encroached on by carbon copies, budgets, and inept church school teachers. I could give a clarion call to the minister to be the minister, as the church is to be the church; and cap the climax by allocating all financial matters to a business administrator, all telephones and letters to a host of efficient secretaries, all committee meetings to something known as a "responsible laity," and all denominational program materials to limbo.

Can you not picture the utopia this would conjure in manifold ministerial breasts, including your own? At last we could get back to real morning devotions to start the day right, not the hasty scriptural snack to which we now seem confined. A productive but useful morning in the study would then follow. Think how rich our sermons would become. And we should, at last, have time to keep up with biography, with fiction, with history, as well as with all the branches of theology. No longer could the names of either Barth or Hemingway make us cringe. We should finally be able to quit pretending that we know who Heidegger is, why Toynbee is to be regarded with suspicion, and what an affluent society really means. When our imagined afternoon is considered, what Christian bliss indeed to make those hospital calls upon patients awaiting eagerly our attentive ear and reassuring word. Later in the afternoon we may rescue a marriage or two, save an adolescent from a criminal career, cure a morphine addict, and a few other similar but daily successes. And when evening comes, then above all we may finally not neglect our home but may play parchesi and backgammon with our adoring family gathered around us. Perhaps one evening telephone call, from some inept committee chairman, could be tolerated. After all, he could simply be told what to do and to take the responsibility for it. But no more. At bedtime what bliss to look back and thank God that one has, at last, had a day worthy of a minister's vocation: plenty of prayer, plenty of study, plenty of service, plenty of family, and no conflicting demands from any person or group. With such a day behind one, he could give up not only tranquillizers but also his last vestige of relevance to the needs of today's world.

If we should go back over this utopia with a realistic eye, the previous conclusions must at least be qualified. Our devotions go barren after ten minutes because we are awaiting a call from the hospital or the forms to make out our income tax. Our study is great for an hour; but then, right in the middle of Toynbee, we have to plunge into the consideration of new hymnals. The calls and counseling in the afternoon find one person bitter, another dependent, another recalcitrant; with few if any notches cut into the pastoral gun by tea time. And as to the evening, which child would drop dead first if father had time to play anything, let alone parchesi?

The tone of these remarks so far may appear to be realistic almost to the point of cynicism and exaggerated almost to the point of caricature; and I freely admit, on points like this, a certain initial predilection for excess. Although I shall not continue in such an extreme strain, it is simply my experience that, where some meaningful analysis of administration is concerned, nothing succeeds like excess—at least in getting attention.

Let me put in a quite different way one fact that has already been stated in another way but perhaps so that it sailed by before the reader could grasp it. That fact is that what ministers say they like to do is precisely what they do alone and by themselves without having to consult anyone but God, and that what they dislike doing is consulting and winning and relating to other people in order to get something done. They like preaching and pastoral care. They need not consult a congregational vote concerning the subject for the next sermon, nor have a committee diagnose a particular parishioner's spiritual needs before they make a call. If they succeed, it is they (and of course God) who did it. If they fail, well, sometimes they fail, sometimes they are not appreciated, and sometimes the people were not ready. But succeed or fail, they have not been compelled to consult. The Lone Ranger rides off into the evening haze.

They do not like administering and executing. Whatever the specific task, the one thing that cannot be done with it is to move simply and plainly from one's conviction to getting the thing done. A committee has to be called or consulted, and have its shins barked and its theology redecorated. A moribund society has to be revived, since even the Lord is manifestly not powerful enough to kill it. Even a letter cannot be answered without consulting the encyclopedia, the church secretary, the chairman of the board, or the Heidelberg Catechism. A thousand consultations shall fall at thy administrative right hand, and ten thousand executive encounters at thy left. And they shall make thee tetched.

I simply see no escape from the conclusion that, at least in our ministerial dreams if not in our practice, our patron saint is a combination of Narcissus and Hotspur. We want to do it alone, and we do not want to be distracted by other people's opinions. Perhaps the sign on the ideal ministerial door, if it were honest, would read, "No waiting; painless extractions; privacy assured." To be sure, this is a rather odd motto for the ministry of a church that professes to serve the world, and to do so through a Living Word carried and conveyed by a fellowship and in which priesthood is somehow conceived to be a universal function and not an aristocratic prerogative.

If I thought the distortion we now confront were only a small one, I should not be obliged to bring in the dangerous big guns of satire. But the twisting seems massive. Tinkering will not do. Something fundamental is wrong. And while I do not propose to set it all aright, I do want to take as clear a look at it as possible. For I believe that a hatred and distaste for everything lumped together as administration can be as severe an enemy of ministry as can the absence of the gospel message.

Administration and Poor Administration

In the argument that I shall make from here on, defending administering by interpreting it as no less important than preaching, I shall not, however, attempt to defend everything going under the name of administration. For some administration is poor not because it is administration but because it is poor. And it, for the most part, is what gives rise to the general image that ministers have when administration is mentioned. We may symbolize this by the cartoon image of the minister with rolled-up sleeves cranking the mimeograph machine.

In normal situations, as a matter of fact, this is not a proper image of administration but of the failure of good administration. For it suggests that the minister has accepted, or been beaten into, a hired-man position around the church. If anything involves work, "we pay him, don't we?" But the fact is that masochism of some type, even the ecclesiastical, is needed to perpetuate such practices. So far as routine duties are concerned, no minister may properly conceive of himself as either a hired hand or a fall guy. Why is he cranking that machine? One reason might be that he cannot tolerate a sense of obligation to anyone; and if he got a good volunteer to handle the machine, he would have to be grateful; and since grateful feelings embarrass him, he cranks the machine, finally, to prevent the embarrassment of gratitude. Another reason might be that he can not bear to request paid secretarial help; for this would involve a need for more money; and thus he would lose his reputation for being such a "spiritual" person. It is also thoroughly possible that none of these Freudian revelations of inverted pride is nearly so important as his not being smart enough to ask the right people in the right way at the right time for the right things in the right tone of authority. But, whatever the reasons, he is not merely doing himself a disservice and building up a greater head of steam against something he thinks of as administration. He is also selling out the ministry of Word and sacraments. He shows that, whatever the reason, he has failed to interpret his function to his people, has not elicited their support and their service to enable him to perform the function; and in this instance has failed to get the people doing the mimeographing who ought to be doing it. This is not administration but poor administration.

We must, then, reject the mimeographing image of the ministry. But we must do so for the right reason. The reason is certainly not that the minister is too good to be caught mimeographing. Suppose that the time is Saturday evening, and that Mrs. Jones, who was to have mimeographed the Sunday bulletin as usual on Saturday afternoon, got a pain about noon and was taken to the hospital. Under these circumstances the pastor might very well be behind the machine for this occasion. No necessary function in the life of the church is foreign to him or beneath him, under special circumstances. But that is very different from making mimeographing normative.

Servanthood, which is so focal in our conception of ministry, always involves a proper relationship between two kinds of elements. On the one hand, since it seeks to serve where service is needed, nothing that serves needs is in principle beneath its notice. But on the other hand, as the notion of "waiter at table" that lies behind the servanthood idea is analyzed, it is clear that some kind of covenant about types of service offered and expected under normal conditions is essential. If there is no covenant, then service is forced into slavery. And if there is no spirit of commitment to meeting needs but only acceptance of specific tasks, then only a job is being performed and there is no servanthood. The minister is not too good to mimeograph. But his covenant should normatively be to things other than mimeographing.

Undoubtedly some poor administration comes from plain inefficiency, fancy laziness, and plain or fancy lack of self-discipline that fails to get some things, like correspondence, done when they ought to be done. But for much of it the motives seem far more complex and hidden.

For instance, let us take a quick look at Pastors A, B, C, and D, each of whom has just reported to a friend, with a mixture of pride and petulance, that he was not home a single night last week. Each complains about committees, conferences, and meetings. But when we take a good subsurface look at Pastor A, we find that he simply dropped in on three of the meetings—"They expect it of their pastor," he says. And on each occasion the chairman of each meeting, at the beginning, middle, and end, has expressed profuse thanks to the pastor for his presence and his wisdom, without which apparently dire events would have occurred. It takes no great psychological penetration to recognize that in Pastor A's case his petulance about meetings is a bit feigned provided the correct doses of adulation have been doled out.

Pastor B looks at his meetings a bit differently. He fears that one committee, left to itself, might vote against God; another against the prayer book; and the third against the Republican party. Of course, if asked, he would deny that he regards himself as the indispensable man. But the fact is that the load he carries rather obsessively and narcissistically on his shoulders is the one thing that prevents him from admitting his secret self-judgment: that he is a lightweight.

The secret and unacknowledged fear of Pastor C, we find upon analysis, is that the committees will get along beautifully in his absence; and then where will he be? Pastor D, we find, attends the meetings, and then complains privately about them, because if they were not around to distract him, he would be compelled to face an evening with his family, or to make needed calls on parishioners, or to read a book. These latter possibilities all being, under the surface, too dire to contemplate, it is the meetings that receive his attention. Indeed, what would any of these ministers do with their aggressive impulses if there were no committees to blame them on?

There is, I believe, a little bit of each one of these hypothetical pastors in each of us. Some of our own poor administration comes not from ordinary inefficiency but from more subtle motivations about which we have not come clean. Can you, if the situation really calls for it, leave the telephone temporarily unanswered? Do you, in chairing a meeting, find yourself pouring oil instead of helping to clarify conflicts because you yourself feel threatened by the very fact of the conflicts? Do you use your car inefficiently not because you are incapable of plotting out an efficient round of trips but because it has become your real "castle," the one place where you can get away from immediate requests without feeling guilty? Do you complain privately about your secretary—who performs miracles already with the bad syntax of your dictation, but who cannot quite make you sound like Winston Churchill— because, if you took trouble with your syntax, you would be like an ordinary man and not a great spiritual leader? Do you build up inner resentment quietly when asked to do something unreasonable by someone from denominational headquarters, instead of taking the risk of being honest and open and saying no? There is a little bit of yes to each of these, and similar, questions in us all.

All of us are involved to some degree, then, in partially poor administration. But the astonishing fact is that our general conception of administration is determined by what is poor, not by what is good. When we considered preaching, we saw, in contrast, that our image comes from preaching performing its best and proper function, not from its distortions. Now, with administration, we find that pathology provides the norm. That is why the distortion is massive, and why our analysis both of poor or distorted administration and of positive and proper administration is so important. We turn now to the positive image of administering.

75

Administering as Commitment Through Group

Our proper conception of administration, like our image of preaching, has its modern starting point in the Reformation. It stems from the two closely related doctrines of the universal priesthood of believers and the universality of Christian vocation. Thus, from this perspective, administration was not invented solely in the twentieth century, and it was not a device of the devil. The meaning behind it is, in our Protestant tradition, just as important an interpretation of the meaning of ministry as is the preaching image.

Put in cartoon form, the image is this: a pastor standing slightly behind two other Christians, with a hand on the shoulder of each person.

The first fact that strikes us in this image is that there is a group, and that the group is made explicit. Whatever the persons may be assumed to be looking at, they are all looking at the same thing, in the same direction. It is not simply that they have a common goal. More basically, their actual perceptions share commonality. Further, there are three persons, thus clearly a group. Thus, any false interpretation that might arise if there were but two persons—master and servant, day and night, or even sexual connotations—are set aside by the presence of three. Since three is not a rounding-off number, as Carl Jung has reminded us, three is the proper symbolic number for this group; for they and their task are by no means rounded off. It is a group that is incomplete and with rough edges, just as it should be.

Second, it goes almost without saying that the members of the group are all shown on the same level. We saw that this same point was implicit in the preaching image. Here it is explicit, and there can be no mistake.

Third, the image acknowledges functional differences among the group members but no distinction as to basic task. There is no sentimental groupiness about everyone being as competent about everything as everyone else just because all are on the same level. The minister is shown with his hand on the shoulders of the others. His function is to provide a necessary and welcome guidance. But one may equally turn this statement about and say that the minister acknowledges he cannot move on alone. The need of minister for people, and of people for minister, is equal. And the basic task can be understood only in the light of what they can do together, even though functions are different.

Perhaps someone might want to make something out of the minister's being a bit behind the laymen. In my cartoon the reason for this is that otherwise he would have to be a contortionist to get his hands on their shoulders, or would have to embrace them, neither of which alternatives gives quite the proper impression. Perhaps there is symbolic significance in the minister's being just a bit behind. The people are the frontier contacts with the world. At least collectively, they know far more of the details of the world with its sin and sorrow than he individually can know. Perhaps it is proper for him to be taught by them about the world they all, as a group, seek to serve and to save.

When we look at the combined elements of this image, I contend that we are viewing the essence of ministry as administering in exactly the sense that the image of open-Bible–pulpit–preacher gave us the image of preaching.

In tracing the roots of this image of administering, it is clear that the biblical conception of servanthood would come first. Yet it is not serving that makes this image unique; for all proper images of the ministry also demonstrate forms of serving. The unique aspect of the present image comes from the Reformation juncture of universal priesthood and Christian vocation.

The universal priesthood of believers was partly a constructive and partly a polemical doctrine. It did not mean, as has sometimes been hastily and wrongly assumed, that every Christian is his own all-sufficient priest. It did mean two things: that a specially designated hierarchy as a channel of access to God was rejected; and that, under some conditions, any Christian might properly serve as priest to any other. Priesthood in general implies mediation or linkage. The Reformers were too wise to deny that linkage might be needed, even by ordained ministers. But they denied possession of a linkage function by a priestly class. Thus the whole conception of linkage, or human mediation, or of priesthood was changed from a status notion to a functional one. The paradox involved in this redefinition was very effectively

77

prefigured in Paul's statements about burden bearing. Christians are to bear one another's burdens; but as he becomes able, every Christian is to bear his own burden.

Perhaps the thrust of the universal priesthood doctrine may appear more clearly if we think of some partial parallels. For instance, except for the unfamiliarity of the term, it would not be inappropriate today to call the best relationships in small groups of workers "the foremanship of all workers." We might even conceive of the "universal vice-presidency of all junior executives." Bernard M. Loomer once spoke of the "deanship of all instructors." Such terms connote something quite different from the "dictatorship of the proletariat," the "kingship of all lords," or the aristocracy of everybody who is not "in trade." They do not deny the importance of a focusing or guiding or leading function, and of its incarnation in foremen, vice-presidents, or deans. But just as the foreman's function can be performed only through and in cooperation with the workers, so the function of the workers can be performed only as they acknowledge and responsibly live up to the "foreman" dimensions of their jobs.

The related Reformation doctrine was Christian vocation, which also had a constructive and a polemical dimension. Polemically it was denied that only priests are called by God to what they are doing. Instead, every Christian is called to his total functions in life: what he does in the church, what he does at home, and above all what he does in his work. True, the modern use of the term "vocation" as a synonym for working occupation is a serious distortion. But it was certainly the most radical aspect of the Reformation vocation doctrine to link a Christian's calling explicitly with the way he earned his living. His vocation was a significant, and often the major, aspect of his ministry.

Every Christian, asserted the vocation doctrine, is called to active ministry. From church and Bible, through Word and sacraments, he receives the grace that makes him a believer. But the life of a believer is ministry. The inevitable response to a true "hearing" is some kind of action—first in worship, to be sure, but then just as surely in service of God through serving the needs of the world. The Christian may of course go out from church and testify to others in the world, verbally, of the riches of his faith.

He may perform special kinds of service, philanthropic, foot-washing, or their equivalent. But the radical declaration of the Reformation doctrine, while not denying either foot-washing or verbal testimony, was that a man's principal ministry, in response to his vocation, was in the course of his common life. If he is husband and father, let him minister there through the quality of his common service to his family. If he is an artisan, let him glorify God and serve mankind by the excellence of his work and its products. To serve God he does not have to dream up some special daily good deed. Let him do well what he normally does in the common life, and this will be the principal indication of his hearing God's particular call to him, and of carrying out his particular ministry as a result.

With universal priesthood and Christian vocation both in mind, let us backtrack to the administering image and reexamine it. A minister and two other Christians, with the minister's hands on the shoulders of the others, all facing in the same direction. In the image universal priesthood is in the foreground. All are committed to the same basic task; but there are differences of function among them; and each needs the others if the common task is to be performed. There can be no lone-wolfishness or going-it-alone. Ministry involves commonality of basic task and mutuality of appreciation of different functions in performing that task. In terms of functions performed, the other Christians may be said to be as truly ministering to the minister as he may be said to be ministering to them. All three, jointly, seek to minister in Christ's name to the world that stands beyond them.

But the Christian vocation notion, while not in the forefront of this image, is not absent from it either. How does each person express his response to God's call? What the image does show is that each person expresses it according to his gifts or abilities or assignments, that is, functionally. The image denies that any one means of functional expression is inherently better than any other. Do what you are capable of doing—provided that it is seen as movement toward performance of the common task—and you are fulfilling your vocation.

Since the cartoon image is not a filmstrip, it does not go on to show the three Christians about their specific duties in the world.

But that is implied. They do not simply stay in church. They do not remain as a literal proximate group twenty-four hours a day. Each goes out into the world to exercise his vocation, partly on special service, to be sure, but mainly through his participation in the common life, which is also ministry, if he so understands it.

When we look at the image from the point of view of the ordained minister, which is unapologetically our focus in this book, it becomes clear why this is an image of administering. For what the minister wants to get done cannot possibly be done by him alone. It must be done through and with—above all, in consultation with—other Christians. Precisely who should do what is not, so to speak, fixed in advance of the consultation. If the situation were always such that the minister allocated responsibilities to the others, then one assumes that he could go happily back to his lone-wolf duties except for the occasional periods of referral. But the actual situation is not like that. The result of the consultation may be to give him new responsibilities, or to give him a new sense of responsibility about guiding the others in the exercise of their functions. The results of true consultation are never wholly predictable. Thus real consultation is an enemy of that kind of mental economy that wants to know, now and forever, precisely what pigeonholes are for what pigeons. The administering image declares such a compulsion to be incompatible with true ministry.

There is one additional way in which all this may be put from the perspective of the ordained minister. The image tells us that the unique thing about the minister's vocation is his responsibility for guiding the Christian vocations of others. But if this is so, and if, as is also true, he is minister of the Word and sacraments, then it must follow that guiding the Christian vocations of others is as indispensable an aspect of receiving responsibly the Word and sacraments as is preaching or pastoral care. If administering is being properly done, one does not, therefore, leave it in order to get back to the true ministry of the Word when he enters the pulpit or the study or the counseling room. Either administering is an essential mode of ministry of the Word, or else the Reformers were entirely wrong about universal priesthood and Christian vocation.

The Psychology of Administering

So far as time and insights permit, we have demonstrated in summary the theological bases of administration as an essential dimension of ministry. It is evident that the psychological attitude making possible the risk of investing one's most precious projects unto others in consultation involves some basic surrender of the notion that ministry is what one does by himself. Conversely, inability so to invest, or the more frequent grumbling about the investment, are rooted in an attitude that at some level still regards basic consultation as an enemy of ministry.

This point brings us full circle to the reported fact that what ministers most dislike is their administrative and executive duties. In attempting to correct this point of view, I have so far drawn on two main lines of argument. The first is the injunction to efficiency in administration, lest administration be wrongly equated with poor administration. The second has been to give some vision, with a theological searchlight, of the context in which administration should be understood. I turn now, third and finally, to one additional line of argument in attacking the prejudice against administration; namely, a direct attack to expose the partly hidden motives of the administration-hater.

He who dislikes administration has a feeling, somewhere inside him, that this sort of thing is "secondhand." There is no direct pristine line from pastoral intention to ecclesiastical performance (as there seems, deceptively, to be in regard to preaching and pastoral care). Instead, one has to enter a labyrinth. Instead of the committee's clear, well-informed, and spontaneous formulation of a plan that executes perfectly and automatically what the minister had in mind, one has to listen to that garrulous Mr. Jones, whose knowledge of the Bible is abysmal and whose preoccupation with the surgery he had two years ago is unflagging, and to Mrs. Smith, who has always found some odd thing in some odd church magazine that she thinks we might try here and which is always irrelevant to the business at hand, and to Dr. Brown, who has a big income himself but seizes every opportunity to ensure that the minister shall prove his piety by his poverty. How could God conceivably believe that a true ministry should involve working with committees that contain people like this? In putting it this way, a minister is of course saying that he is too important and his time is too valuable to waste in educating or changing or shepherding people while he is engaged in consulting them. Thus he has no inner readiness for consultation at all. He may talk about encounter, but he demonstrates his ignorance of its meaning. There can be no I-Thou relationships with rubber stamps or sycophants.

Another related thing we may say about the administration-hater is that risks make him fearful. To commit one's time and energies, and his best interpretations and arguments, to decision in which others share must inevitably be an anxiety-inducing business unless one has a bit of a psychological free-swing about him. But one can have this kind of attitude only if, in fact, he is not inwardly compelled to feel defensive about his work and its results. If one feels securely that he has been given a treasure, and the treasure is not of the kind that is dissipated by sharing, then he can risk (within some prudent and intelligent limits) freely and even gladly. Psychologically speaking, he learns that even his aggressive energies are meant for the service of God, no less than his tenderness and his concern. But if he feels threatened, he cannot risk. And in that case his first question to himself should be not how to get out of the administrative involvement but exactly what does put him on the defensive. There surely must be some connection between the fear of risk and what I believe to be the fact: that the administration-haters are also the ministers who complain most bitterly about the reluctance of laymen to assume responsibility.

There is likely to be also, among the disapprovers of administration, quite a bit of perfectionism. There is always a certain nobility of aim in even the most disastrous perfectionism. What one does should be done well, it says. But it turns out ordinarily that what one wants to be able to do well is what no one else can evaluate; and hence the motive behind the perfectionism is not excellence of performance but freedom from appraisal. Of all the aspects of ministry, administering is that in which appraisal of the minister is most open and unconcealed. The minister who cannot receive appraisal with some kind of objective but serious ear is in a poor position to guide his people to find their Christian vocation, for that too rests upon appraisal.

Finally, I think there is a kind of "merit-badge" psychology at work in those who dislike administration. In a way one can, after a sermon or a pastoral interview, attach another bar to his pin. He knows he has been a minister; he preached or acted as shepherd. But with a committee or a pile of letters, no merit badge. In the terms of Gestalt psychology, one has not got "closure." Everything is open-ended. Now, without necessarily being against merit badges in the proper setting, which is for Boy Scouts, for adults to have their professional self-respect dependent upon their equivalent suggests at the least some deep interior doubt about the integrity of one's commitment. On this point, as on the others, I do not intend merely to cast aspersions on those who hate administration (for some part of all of us feels this way), but rather to compel our rethinking of our motivations.

One other kind of comment is needed on the psychology of administration. No doubt you have already been thinking, "But what about those ministers who get so delightedly involved in the machinery and the wheels that they become no good at all about preaching, pastoral care, or anything else?" I would agree that this is a serious question, most of all in American churches. My argument for the essentiality of administering is in no way an invitation to neglect sermons, pastoral care, or anything else that is crucial in a total ministry.

But just what, from a psychological point of view, happens with the man whose delight is in the law of wheels turning round? He has, if I may use a psychoanalytic term, demonstrated that we may have "reaction-formations" in the ministry. In psychoanalysis a reaction-formation is said to appear when the automatic defense that is brought to bear against something that cannot be admitted takes a form precisely the opposite of what is being denied, as when a compulsive neatness appears on the surface to ward off riotous interior desires to be messy, or when effusive sweetness in words covers up an unadmitted desire to dominate. The minister wholly occupied with turning wheels is, in all probability, distracting himself from the emptiness he believes he would find if he took his mind off wheels and put it onto ministry. Even if such a person is called a good administrator, I believe that this is seldom true according to the criteria suggested in the present discussion. He is not so much working through and with other people in a common task, about which he bears particular kinds of responsibilities, as he is keeping himself so busy that he need not ask what is unique about his vocation. Thus, he is least of all prepared to understand the present discussion. In contrast, the minister with a bit of administration-hating in him is far more likely to make enough change in his outlook to become a proper administrator as an aspect of his total ministry.

Limitations of the Administering Image

Finally, let me remind you that the administering image, valuable as it is when it is rightly understood, is still a cross-section, a cartoon, that has temporarily neglected some things in order to give proper emphasis to other things. Let us make sure that we beat off in advance some possible misinterpretations.

Someone might say, "How do we know that this picture is a Christian one? Could it not just as well be a picture of a democratic society?" As stated, it could indeed be so. But this is no handicap in a cartoon if we grasp both its intent and its context. Indeed, the preaching image simply showed an open book, and we had to imagine the right context in order to see that this book was manifestly the Bible. To try to make clear our administering image, of course we might put all three men on their knees. But not only would that require the minister to be a contortionist in putting his hands on the shoulders of the others; it would also mean that the men would have to bow their heads, and the reference in the actual image to their work to be done in the world might be clouded. Perhaps each layman could be carrying a Bible; or one layman a Bible and the other some symbol of service such as a cup. Yet all such suggestions really miss the point. No cartoon image can present the whole context in which it is to be understood. To try to make it do so makes it lose its power.

In similar vein, someone else may ask, "How do we really know the difference between the minister and the others, when they are all dressed alike?" If it suits the sartorial aspects of the fellowship, I suppose I can concede a robe or a reversed collar. But certainly not a frock coat. Such queries could be endless. Why are they all men? Why not a woman and a child? An older person? Someone who is ill? All such questions do indeed remind us that we are dealing with a cartoon, with an attempt at emphasis that must, for the time being, leave certain other things unexplicit. But this procedure is, in actual fact, the way the human mind works—from a vague, diffuse, and blobby kind of general perception, in the direction of increasing specificity, and then back to a much more accurate and articulated whole. Our cartoons are neither the first nor the last word. But they are very important somewhere in the middle.

I conclude with a rather risky word about God. A great part of the content of our Christian faith declares that God, although free to do otherwise, did actually create us in his own image, which includes some significant measure of freedom and of capacity to love; that we have individually and collectively misused our freedom and not cultivated our love capacity; that an astoundingly radical procedure was used to get us humans out of our predicament; and that it is the constant privilege and duty of the church to testify to the salvation already wrought and to bring all men and ourselves to receive it. But when we look at actual existence, we have to begin theologizing, that is, acknowledging the complications. And at that point there is no reflective Christian who has not at some time asked the question, "Was God out of his mind to entrust this most precious treasure to people like us and churches like ours?" And if he has answered the question rightly, he has finally said, "Yes, we are as bad as that; but God was willing to risk it, and he must know what he is doing."

If even God felt it wise and right and essential to risk his purposes and his love through fallible human instruments, who is a minister to be unwilling to acknowledge that his ministry must be risked through fallible human beings who are, in actual fact, no more fallible than he?

5

The Ministry as Teaching

In spite of the emphasis placed by the Protestant Reformers, especially Calvin, upon the function of teaching, no image of the ministry as teaching—apart from preaching—has come down to us from that age.

The reasons for this fact are historically complex. Most obvious is that teaching at all levels and with all subject matter came to be done in "schools," institutions with their own type of organization even when in or related to churches. The people who worked in schools became "teachers." Thus "teaching" and "teacher" could not, like preaching and preacher, be used to designate something unique to the minister. And when ministers ceased to think of themselves as teachers, it was only a step to think of their communicative function as other than teaching.

There was also in the background rebellion against the approximately eight hundred years in which the teaching of people by the church had been much more by symbolism—architecture, the Mass, and the like—than by direct discourse. Not without justice, the Reformers believed that this was an obscurantist policy. They stressed communicating the message of the Bible; and while they spoke of this procedure as both preaching and teaching, it was preaching that was unique to the ministry. And as the Protestant centuries went on, even teaching, if done by the minister, was ordinarily referred to as preaching.

Perhaps another reason for the absence of a Reformation image of the minister as teacher (apart from preacher) was the Protestant concern for study of the Bible by all Christians. This led on the one side to the development of schools at all levels, and on the other side to a new kind of reliance upon the family as the primary Christian school. In relation to all such enterprises the ordained minister was, in fact, what we should today call an administrator or supervisor. The notion of teaching, however, even to this day, has been associated with direct encounter. The facilitation of learning was not thought of as teaching, as I believe it should be.

But if we look at what the Reformation tried to do in fact, and not merely at its partly polemical images, it becomes perfectly possible to construct an image of the minister as teacher—which the Reformation should have made explicit. Here was the extraordinary claim that the Bible should be read in every home in the vernacular, so the people of all ages could understand its meaning. If the head of the household could not read, let him be so taught. Let him not be arbitrary in his understanding of what he read. In the church he may get corrective instruction about his own interpretations. But what he hears in church is not a substitute for his own study and his leadership of his family in such study.

An image could have been constructed in which the ordained minister is shown in a private residence, seated beside the father, with the rest of the family grouped around. A Bible would rest upon the table in front of minister and father, and both would have their eyes upon it. The best account available of this kind of ministerial practice is contained in Richard Baxter's *The Reformed Pastor*, published at the middle of the seventeenth century.

Viewed in retrospect, the contribution of Protestant ministers to this kind of at-home Bible study and instruction is probably as significant historically as their work in founding schools at many levels. But it was "quiet work." It seemed not to lend itself to an image as did the function of preaching. Further, was it "teaching"? It was instruction about instructing! Even to this day, every school administrator knows that his former classroom colleagues regard him as having deserted "teaching" in favor of "educational administration." They will concede him the title of "educator," but not of "teacher."

My argument is, then, that the activities of the Reformation warranted an image of the minister teaching—when shown as instructing a group (focally the family but also other kinds of groups) on how to continue their instruction and learning. The fact that such an image did not appear is due to the factors that have been mentioned and no doubt to many others that have not. But from Reformation practice the significant fact is that the minister's exercise of his teaching function is instructing about instructing—and not doing all the instructing himself.

It may even be that to early Protestants the New Testament, especially the four Gospels, was an unconscious barrier against creating an actual image of the ministry as teaching. In the Gospels, Jesus is called "teacher" far more than any other term, especially when it is recognized that the appellation of "master" was also intended in early Protestant translations to mean "teacher." But what was Jesus doing when he sent out the twelve and the seventy? He taught them before they went; and he appraised their work, and their response to it, upon their return. Was this "teaching"? I certainly believe so. But the obtrusiveness of his own direct public speaking in the New Testament put the Reformers off about seeing it this way.

As Protestant time has gone on, the categories hardened about what is preaching, teaching, or evangelizing. Preaching became associated with the context of worship; so that it takes a strong reminder that preaching may also be evangelistic, i.e., the message addressed to those who do not share the assumptions of the preacher. Teaching became associated with "preparation," i.e., what is done before the context of worship to prepare for it—thus tending to exclude the context of worship as actual teaching or instruction. Evangelizing tended to be defined in theory as dealing with nonbelievers, but in actual practice to be associated with a special kind of worship context to which the nonbeliever must conform if he was present at all.

Some conclusions seem warranted from these linguistic developments. The main one is that teaching, in effect, gets excluded from relationship with worship except as possible preparation. The notion that worship could not only stimulate the desire for learning, but itself be a new step in learning, seems to disappear. If any "conviction" appears, then what has gone on is not "teaching" but "preaching." Such views obviously keep teaching in an anteroom.

The catechisms of early Protestantism were creeds designed for instructional purposes. Their title was derived from a Greek word meaning to "sound" or to "resound." Later, when it was seen that systematic study of the functions of church and ministry was necessary, it was logical to use the word "catechetics" to apply to teaching and learning. This term—with its feeding back precisely what had originally been "sounded"—had many negative implications in the development of effective teaching methods, and of course today has been virtually discarded.

In the first centuries of Christianity, catechumens were adult converts who had to undergo long and arduous instruction before being admitted to the church through baptism. When Christianity became official, the time and instruction were cut more and more. In a sense, the catechisms of early Protestantism were attempts to return to the ways of the early church, for which such teaching and learning were very important. But by the time "catechetics," as the study of instruction, became a theological discipline in the seventeenth or eighteenth century, a curious reversal had taken place, and most of the talk was about dealing with children. Since then, systematic instruction of anybody but children has become a rarity.

The "Repeat-After-Me" Image

By somewhere along in the nineteenth century, I suggest that the image in vogue of the minister as teacher was about like this. There was a frock-coated and stiff-collared minister standing before a group of starched and uncomfortable boys, he asking questions to which they were to give precise answers—such as, "Who made you? Answer: God."

At first glance, beginning with the collars, the image is wholly repellent to us today. The boys cannot think for themselves or put it in their own words. They must give the book answer. While the minister may be kindly enough to help them with a forgotten word, he is not aiding them to think out its meaning in their terms. He is a relatively impersonal examiner rather than a teacher.

How they actually were induced to memorize is not shown in the image, nor is there any revelation of what the memorizations mean to the boys.

Obviously I can hold no brief for the collar, the sheer memorizing, the lack of authentic exchange, and the like that this image contains. But there are two facts about it which we seem to have discarded too easily. The first is the simple fact that the minister himself has some place in the teaching process—no matter who got the material into the heads of the boys. The second fact is that some kind of examinational procedure is regarded as natural and normal.

Of course I am for modern theories and methods of instruction, with exchange between teacher and students and with students encouraged to take all the initiative of which they are capable. But where in the church today is anybody, with his own consent, ever really examined about what he has learned? The purpose of such an appraisal may indeed be to make possible a decision, as in connection with passing or failing a formal course. But if that exhausts its function, poor teaching is taking place. An examination in itself, no matter what its nature, is to help the student toward better capacity for self-appraisal, getting appropriate confidence in his strong points and learning about the weak ones that need more work. Thus, a proper examination is a part of the learning process, and not merely a formal testing of what it has accomplished to date. I suggest that this notion, in however backhanded a way, was present in our frock-coated minister, and that we should recover it and bring its attitudes and methods up to date.

The minister, further, although he could not possibly sit down at length with every child or small group of children and teach them all that they should learn, was nevertheless involved in the teaching process. Presumably it was parents, and then later church school teachers, who got the material into the boys initially. But even today I believe these lay teachers might go at their task differently if they knew that the product of their efforts was to be appraised, in some proper way, and that this appraisal too was part of the teaching and learning process.

In the previous section, building from the activities of the

Reformation, I suggested that the image of instructing the instructors is valid if brought up to date as to method. In the present section I have argued that the image of appraising, in proper ways, as a part of teaching, and with the minister having some part in it, is important. I see no reason why these two general kinds of function are any less proper "teaching" than direct instruction of an individual or a small group.

The Motherly Teacher

I am not sure when it began to happen in a big way—probably not until the latter half of the nineteenth century—but the image of the real teacher of children became the motherly person in the Sunday school. My own entire career in Sunday school had such motherly persons as teachers. One of them, the best, is still vivid in my memory. She stood for no nonsense like spitballs; yet in spite of the authority we respected, she was kind and honestly interested in each of us, and we knew it. If we forgot to bring a verse for the day, she would give us a hand while exercising some precautionary scolding against next Sunday's verse. Of course I remember my fellow student who brought in "Jesus wept." But he could not place it in the biblical numbers game. It may have helped that this teacher was a good friend of my mother, and that we had family social affairs together on occasion.

The image of the motherly person actually trying to get it into the heads of the boys was an improvement in some obvious respects over the frock-coat image. It was directly concerned with the learning process and did not concentrate on testing the results. The motherly person was there to nurture, firmly but kindly, at a period in American cultural development when a man would not have been believable in this role with children. Like my own teacher, she represented a movement toward acknowledging the boyishness of boys or the girlishness of girls; but being a step removed from the actual mother, she could be firmer and more systematic.

Like the Sunday school system itself, this motherly-person image was a recognition that, in terms of method, the family could not be counted on to do the whole needed teaching job along with services of worship. This was realism, for the function of the family was changing; and here was recognition of the fact, even though there may have been little sociological theory behind it.

Having said good things for the motherly-person image, however, we must also note some deficiencies. To begin with, it is vaguely anti-intellectual. If her attitude is good and she follows the written instructions, she can teach what is needed—even if she knows nothing about "theology." In addition, the motherly person is teaching, but she is not concomitantly learning except through reading her lesson materials. And indeed, as the Sunday schools developed, their administrators as well as teachers were laymen; and only on some special retreat did the teachers have direct contact with the ordained minister about the content of their task. There is the strong suspicion, in a look at the image, that the minister has unloaded teaching altogether because it is only an anteroom function.

It is a good thing indeed that men as well as women, young women as well as matrons, and talented older people of both sexes have also been engaged in the teaching enterprises of the churches. The shift away from fixed male-females roles has helped the churches to get more men engaged where they should be. But the image of church school teaching is still the matronly motherly person; and it requires a secure man to take up that particular cross.

Not a little of the everlasting new curriculums that are issued from the boards of Christian education is, at some level not clearly conscious, aimed at qualifying the motherly-person image in the direction of masculinity and the intellect—without getting rid of Mom altogether. Thumping about theology (which is a masculine discipline) is one way. Beating the table about the Church in capital letters (in capitals it too is male) is another. Maybe the motherly person had it coming to her. But heaven help us if her combination of kindness and firmness is lost, no matter what her theology or her sense of the Great Church. The motherly person was not far from being the Mary of Protestantism. And in actual fact, if we lost her tomorrow, most of our church "educational buildings" would have to be closed.

THE MINISTRY AS TEACHING

The Image of Teaching as "Higher" Calling

One of the genuine achievements of the past quarter-century has been the increase in formal teaching of religion in colleges and universities. In tax-supported schools such teaching must be both competent and fair to all positions; and with rare exceptions it has been so in schools that are related to particular churches. Qualifications for the teachers run high academically. If the teacher does not have an earned doctorate, he is always a bit under suspicion. The earned doctorate in theology is rarely secured with less than seven years of full-time graduate study after the undergraduate college work. Except for surgeons and psychoanalysts, therefore, the school route to becoming a full-time teacher of religion in higher education requires more years than any other field.

Among such teachers who meet all qualifications, there is a growing number who do not wish to be ordained as ministers. In any individual instance such a decision may be excellent, and proper for the person. And as the situation stands at present, the line of division is not between those who are ordained to the ministry and those who are not. The line is, I think, between those who see such teaching as a form of ministry and those who disassociate teaching from ministry and regard religious teaching as a "higher" calling than the ministry.

The higher-calling notion has a long history within the Christian church. Are you a monk, or only a "secular" priest? Are you ordained, or only a friar? Are you a missionary, or only ministering to an established domestic congregation? Are you properly "itinerating," or are you beguiled to settle down somewhere? Even in these modern days I have had long and agonizing interviews and counseling sessions with overseas missionaries who were trying to decide whether, if they exercised ministry back home, they would be recreant to their "higher calling."

Today the higher calling of all higher callings seems to be teaching. For nearly a dozen years I was a member of the Committee to Visit the Divinity School, of Harvard University, a quaint but sometimes useful device dating back to early days when the Commonwealth of Massachusetts had its suspicions about Harvard and exercised them through insisting on such inspection. I "inspected" during the period when Harvard Divinity School moved from an almost moribund institution to the school that it is today.

When the Harvard Divinity School got back on its feet in the early 1950's, it became very "churchy." At the same time, and until this day, a goodly number of its students alleged that they did not want to become "ministers," but rather were interested in becoming "teachers." In this respect Harvard is only an extreme example. Most other theological schools find the same thing in less severe statistical form.

It is certainly possible and, for the particular man, necessary that he take all the training to be a teacher of theology or religion without necessarily becoming an ordained minister. And if he is competent, he is likely to do a great deal of good with his formal teaching in college or university. What he accomplishes may be quite independent of his being ordained or not. What troubles me about the situation is not what happens to this full-time teacher, but the inferiority complex which his training and his (collective) sense of a "higher" calling give to ordained ministers. It is almost as if it were said to the minister: "You aren't equipped to do real teaching; leave that to us."

In a report on "The Nature of the Ministry" to the General Assembly of the United Presbyterian Church in 1964, it was proposed that a teacher be a special kind of minister. It is true that this report met a good deal of opposition and has not been adopted. It suggests, however, the uneasiness of many who do full-time teaching in higher education about separating their status and function from that of ministers in general. My objection is not, of course, to functional specialization, in teaching or any other function. It is using that functional specialism backhandedly to deprive the minister of his own proper commitment to the teaching part of his duties.

A New Teaching Image

I suggest that a new image of the ministry as teaching looks like this. A minister and a layman are seated together at one point of a round table. Seated with them, all round the remainder of the table, are adults of different sexes and ages, but all plainly responsible if part-time teachers. The minister and the lay administrator are jointly instructing the instructors—in dialogue, of course.

When a church educational program is operating effectively, that is the actual situation. The many persons needed for a program must of course be lay men and women. And many aspects of the administration can properly be under lay supervision. But the minister bears ultimate responsibility for the teaching; and unless he has been stampeded away from regarding this supervision as his principal "teaching," he will feel a deep commitment to the entire teaching work of the church through this redefinition of his teaching function.

As more of our local churches become large enough to have more than one minister or professional person on their staff, it is increasingly customary for one of the persons to have functional charge of the Christian education program. Earlier in the century most directors of religious education were not ordained, and nearly all were women. Certainly this is an excellent spot for competent women to serve the church; but of late years more men are holding such positions, and more directors, both men and women, are ordained ministers.

In the new image it should make no difference whether the ordained minister is a man or a woman, a generalist or a specialist minister in education. "Teaching" as such belongs indissolubly with "ministry," special function or no. If we have enough specialists to warrant it, perhaps the image could show two ministers at the round table along with the others. And one might be a woman.

A few props might be inserted into this cartoon image. Of course there should be some curriculum materials on the table. I suggest a couple of hefty Bibles besides. And to show that even very young ages are included in the concern, there might well be some gadget or pictorial device. A newspaper—to show the attempt to connect the gospel with the world—would be appropriate. Perhaps that is sufficient.

In speculating on this image, I suggest that the reader bear in mind that no attempt has been made at a general discussion of Christian education whether in local church or elsewhere. The focus has been on the teaching function inherent in the total work of every ordained minister. I believe that he does far more real teaching than he realizes. I want him to rethink his teaching ministry, and to see it as an essential part of his total ministry.

Whom Shall the Minister Teach?

For the sake of convenience, the locus of the minister's teaching efforts has so far been assumed to be the local church or some extension thereof. That is, it has been assumed that the co-workers and the students are all, at least in some degree, sharers of the basic point of view and commitment that the minister himself has. Certainly this is the center of the teaching work of most ministers.

But no minister, unless immured within his local church structure, is devoid of teaching opportunities in other settings—if he sees them as such and responds appropriately to them. He makes hospital calls; does he, by however indirect means, properly teach what the ministry is, what the church is, and so on, in his hospital relationships? If he belongs to something like the Rotary Club, he does some kind of teaching there, whether for good or ill. In social action projects, too, there is always teaching as well as action.

Unless such situations are invitations to make a formal speech, however, I suggest that ministers today seldom think of the teaching potentialities they afford. One of the factors in my own experience that has made me increasingly regard this as basic to the teaching function of ministry has been my service as theological consultant to mental hospitals, especially the Menninger Foundation.

In hospital parlance a "consultant" is a responsible professional person who appraises the whole situation (be it a case or an idea), engages in responsible mutual discussion about it with the persons regularly in charge, and tries to aid them to improve their ways of understanding the situation and approaching it. The consultant does not "stay." He does not assume the ongoing responsibility.

In my early work as consultant I of course had opportunity to give speeches, to lead special discussion sessions around particular topics, and the like. But I found much that was most significant when I sat in, for instance, in a team case discussion that would have been held anyhow. If I had anything to contribute in shedding light on the situation before us, I could do so. But nobody had to attend a special meeting.

This kind of situation is, I think, something that nearly every minister finds himself in quite often; for the subject matter may be varied, and yet the principle remains. It may be argued that my special status as a consultant facilitates my own way of teaching in such ongoing situations, and that is true. But that only helps things to get started. Something else is needed to make it work.

Conclusion

In summary, my argument is that the minister is, in some sense, a teacher of everybody. To hold this position of course requires that teaching involve the supervision of education, and not be confined to classroom or pulpit-and-pew encounters. Teaching includes the instruction of instructors.

This shift in thinking about teaching is made easier by the new image proposed—a round table, a minister and a lay leader, and other persons, with Bibles and other paraphernalia to show the focus on inquiry. If this image is adopted, it should also aid in closing the gap that now so often exists between ministers and teachers of religion in higher education.

6
The Ministry as Shepherding

In the three aspects of ministry that have been before us so far, we have found focal images that lift up the principal points about meaning. There is a leading image for preaching, one for administering, and one for teaching. But when we turn to the present subject, we find that the focal image is already built into our terminology. We cannot even talk about this aspect of ministry without using the metaphor of shepherd or pastor. There is no way of referring to pastoral care that omits the shepherding analogy. On the face of it, this fact would appear to make our task much easier. If shepherding is such a pervasive image that it has even monopolized the language, surely we can move securely and discard all complex dialectics in our interpretation of the ministry as shepherding.

On the contrary, the situation in fact is more complicated than it first appears. For the words "pastor," or "*poimen*," or "shepherd" have been used in Christian history in two senses, not one. On the one side, the "pastoral" has been conceived as one kind of activity along with others, often as caring for or disciplining or nourishing. But on the other side, the noun "pastor" has been applied as a substantive to the minister, and then anything that he did as pastor was regarded as "pastoring" or "shepherding," thus equating shepherding with anything properly done by a minister. There have been many uneasy compromises between these two notions, both of which seem to me partly right and partly mistaken as they have been stated. Certainly the attempt to equate pastoral care with the total work of ministry is unsatisfactory; for that simply uses an uncriticized metaphor as an imperialistic declaration about the ministry as a whole, and thus concrete meaning is lost from the metaphor. But the other attempt, to make shepherding only a kind of slice of the ministerial pie, is also inappropriate; for it means that there could be nothing seriously pastoral as one preaches or administers, and that is false.

My solution to this problem has been to regard pastoral as a perspective, to note that no event in which a minister is involved is devoid of some pastoral intent and significance, but that in some such events the pastoral motif becomes dominant or of overriding importance. Generally speaking, it is these latter instances to which I would give the name "shepherding" or "pastoral care." I would also limit the term "shepherding" to those situations in which it is possible for the minister to concentrate on the healing, sustaining, or guiding of the person or persons, rather than having primarily, at that point, to protect the interest of the group or the institution as perhaps against that of the person. This distinction does not exclude all "discipline" from pastoral care, but it does exclude such discipline as must sometimes be undertaken whose primary aim is not the reconciliation or restoration of the person.

Modern Precursors of the Shepherding Image

The shepherding image in some form, hopefully the form that will be suggested later, is very probably here to stay. But we need to note that the images and metaphors that were used in the modern revival of concern for pastoral care, with which I am in deep sympathy, have only recently become concerned about shepherding, and for a time were quite different in character. At the very least, this historical fact is a warning that the shepherding image may become irrelevant or meaningless. Any attempts to revive it, such as I myself am making, are likely to be abortive unless they can avoid some dangers into which the image has fallen in the past.

At the turn of the present century, I suspect the dominant image of pastoral care was the minister ringing a doorbell. The writings of that era that were intended for students and for other ministers all stressed pastoral assiduity. If one did not know his sheep, how could he feed them? That very common notion of the time implied that pastoral calls were the knowing, and if the people came to church to hear the sermon that was the feeding. To be sure, in the good books of that general era, such as John Watson's *The Cure of Souls* or Charles E. Jefferson's *The Ministering Shepherd*, there was much wisdom that would be appropriate for any age of ministry. But the image of pastoral care was very much of the doorbell kind. Even if a lecturing or writing parson made a lot of house calls himself, he feared that young ministers would not do so; and in a nice way he tried to enlist them into this faithful activity through testimonial forms of exhortation.

But we now know that, on psychological grounds, exhortations are not the most likely ways of convincing people. They carry a hidden undertone that the thing in itself is really rather dull and has to be dressed up to make it interesting. There were no cases in those days, only anecdotes; and with rare exceptions the anecdotes were all success stories, in line with the hortatory motif. The motion that analysis of a failure might very well elicit much more interest and commitment than an anecdote about success had seemingly occurred to no one. Thus, although we still need to respect the doorbell image, in the sense that the pastor must make himself available to his people and not merely wait in an office until they come, we must reject its hidden assumptions that pastoral work with people is routine, perhaps dull, and certainly not as central to ministry as preaching.

The first competition received by the doorbell image was what I hope Harry Emerson Fosdick will forgive me for calling the "Protestant confessional" image. In a large New York church, and preaching as he always did to try to touch with the gospel the actual needs of people, he found himself besieged by persons seeking interviews. He sought guidance from one of the wise psychiatrists of that day, Thomas W. Salmon; tried to do what he could in helping the people who came; or referred them to others who could help. He also, in an article of the early 1920's, used the phrase, "Protestant confessional." Not long ago I corresponded with him about his intent in using the phrase, and was confirmed in my judgment that he only meant to say that ministers should be as ready of access to persons burdened with guilt and other negative feelings as are Roman Catholic priests.

But the phrase caught on. Busy ministers—and who would admit himself to be otherwise?—suddenly saw entirely new potentialities in talking with people in their studies or offices. Perhaps some used the new image as an excuse to get out of pastoral calling. For the majority, however, the Protestant-confessional image was simply a call to make it clear that ministers had studies where people could talk with them. This became, then, a kind of "interview image," the pastor talking individually with persons who have sought him out. In retrospect, it seems very much like the salesman who has been driving himself frantic traveling over his territory and to whom it suddenly occurs that a lot of his best customers, if given the chance, would like to take the initiative and come to him.

The interview image was appealing in several ways. First, the minister could rid himself of the charge of peddling pills to people who did not want them; for he would interview no one unless the person had sought him out. Second, unlike the home call where the crying baby and the frying bacon could be distracting, it was possible to control the conditions and structure of an interview, thus giving the comforting illusion that one knows what he is about. Third, the general public was just beginning to accord high prestige to several professions for whom the interview is standard procedure, notably psychiatry but also such areas as personnel work, educational guidance, and even social case work. Clinical psychology had not yet come upon the scene in its modern sense. Thus, the pastoral discovery of the interview was temporally correlative with society's discovery that people who interview are important people. Finally, it was tempting to think that, with the more carefully controlled conditions of the interview, something like scientific method could be applied, to the eventual aim of helping many more people.

It is curious that the early days of clinical pastoral education, which has done more than any other movement to foster the present knowledge and skill in pastoral care, actually relied only in part upon interviewing methods and yet made the interview image dominant as the ideal. In actual practice clinical students often began by handling bedpans, were graduated either to making bedside calls or taking a patient for a walk. Such modes of rela-

101

tionship were actually more representative of pastoral encounters than was the formal interview. But so high had the prestige of the interview become that even this practice did not prevent the formation of an ideal interview image.

The first literature that appeared as a result of the new movements, beginning with clinical training but not confined to it, made some use of the interview model although in a vague and diffuse fashion. But the next round of literature, beginning just before World War II, clearly patterned itself on the interview model. Rules were given for "counseling," presupposing the interview situation as normative, with even the hospital call being subjected to the interview image in its essentials. It is probable that Carl R. Rogers' important book, *Counseling and Psychotherapy*, published in the early 1940's and read by many ministers also contributed to use of the interview image.

During World War II and afterward, Harry Bone and I taught a course at Union Theological Seminary in New York. This was entitled "counseling." We were of course committed to use of the case method. When we began, we too had the interview image in the back of our minds. But our students, for the most part, were not operating in situations where they could interview people in any formal sense. We told them, therefore, to report on "contacts" of any kind beyond the realm of personal friendship—calls, apparently casual encounters, and the like. To our great amazement, these materials proved to be rich beyond our hopes. We consciously discarded the interview image and came to terms happily with the fact that 90 percent of the potential helping work of most ministers is done in noninterview situations. Even though my book of 1949 was called *Pastoral Counseling*, and attempted to deal carefully with structured situations symbolized by the term "interview," its principal thrust was in the direction of dynamic analysis of all the kinds of potential helping contacts, formal and otherwise, that the minister has. Thus it was a movement away from the interview image and in the direction of the shepherding image, although it was to be another six or eight years before I developed this latter fully. But in the interim some others, notably Wayne E. Oates, had begun to do so.

102

THE MINISTRY AS SHEPHERDING

Dangers of the Shepherding Image

The clearer it became that we had to develop a fundamental theory of pastoral care, and not just of pastoral counseling, the more it became evident that one of two things had to happen. Either some new central image must be found, or the shepherding image revived and analyzed. Since no possible new central image has been brought forth by any one, to the best of my knowledge, the sole alternative was reconsideration of the shepherding image. Here I rule out of account the small group of ministers who have, in effect, extended the interview image into a psychotherapeutic and even psychoanalytic kind of image; for this simply rules out as insignificant or irrelevant 90 percent of most ministers' opportunities to help. Its defect lies much less in what it tries to assert —careful training, attentiveness to the person, taking adequate time, and the like—than in what it denies—that people can also be helped in many less formal ways and that it is the inherent business of the minister to use the range of ways open to him in his representative capacity.

A reanalysis of the shepherding idea, however, demonstrated at once that there was no clear-cut and agreed-on cartoon comparable to the preaching image of open-Bible–pulpit–preacher. What even the most casual historical inspection showed was two elements—sheep and shepherd—as constants, but with the kind of imageous relationship between them, and combined with additional elements, manifesting great variation. I came to see, on further study, one other common element in all the images—the presence of tender and solicitous concern on the part of the shepherd. But since this is not something that can be portrayed in precisely the same way in all circumstances, it is not the same kind of element as the sheep or the shepherd.

The first task, manifestly, was to disclaim possible elements, meanings, or implications in the shepherd-sheep relationship that conflict with ministry understood in other or larger senses; i.e., using such criteria as we have already tried to summarize in relation to the preaching and administering images. When this is done, some necessary disclaimers become clear at once.

First, the "sheep" in the relationship are to be understood as representing need, and not as inherently stupid, incapable of initiative, or even wholly "innocent." If sheep get lost when they wander away, it can hardly be the spirit of inquiry or adventure that is reprehensible in itself, but rather the ambiguous mixing of this spirit with impulsive immediacy instead of planning, with distrust of the shepherd but fear to come out and say so, and with a rationalization that one's motives are wholly pure and innocent.

Second, the "shepherd" in the relationship is not to be represented as knowing everything, especially about what the sheep ought to do. He may indeed be shown as having such positive qualities as solicitous concern, but he is to be a very human shepherd. He may of course be regarded as an undershepherd, while Jesus Christ is the sole Great Shepherd. But if this image is to be one of ministry through human beings, and thus coordinate with the other images, it must not confuse the shepherd or undershepherd it is demonstrating with Jesus Christ. If there is such confusion of identities, then our shepherd may wrongly be represented as having perfect *agape*, knowing everything, and the like.

Third, the species difference between the human shepherd and the animal sheep is not the point of the image, and must be disclaimed. The sheep are in the image not for their subhuman qualities but on the basis of their need.

Fourth, the image may not properly emphasize collectivity at the expense of individuality. If more than one sheep is shown, it must be clear that pastoral concern for the flock is not exercised merely on a mass basis. This image is probably not the place to adjudicate the relative claims of the lost sheep and the ninety and nine; but as in the parable, it is the single sheep that should be emphasized.

Finally, although the intent of the image deals with concern and attitudes and not with methods and procedures, it ought not to be so presented that skills and procedures appear to be denigrated.

In the light of these necessary disclaimers in the shepherd-sheep relationship, it follows that several kinds of cartoon images that have sometimes been used are incapable of carrying the proper meaning. We cite some of them.

First is the picture of the shepherd with his flock gathered round him. This image is too vague, general, and diffuse, and says nothing about individuality.

Second is the shepherd cradling a single sheep in his arms. This will not do on several counts. It is sentimental; it implies the superior-inferior relationship; and if the sheep is presumed to be injured, it violates the most elementary principle of first aid. That is, it combines sentimentality with a lack of common sense.

Third is a shepherd on foot gazing into the distance where, perhaps, the lost sheep may be glimpsed. The trouble here is that concern seems linked with inattentiveness. How did the sheep get so far away before its absence was discovered? And is it really lost if the shepherd and we can see it?

By this time you may wonder, since the difficulties of getting the right relationship between shepherd and sheep seem so considerable, why we do not leave the pasture and get on with our pastoral urbanization. I abjure you to have patience. The task is not easy, but it is not impossible, and it is worth attempting even in a nuclear age.

The Shepherding Image, Old Style and New

The fundamental intent of any defensible form of the shepherding image is to show the helping concern of the shepherd as somehow relevant to the need of the sheep. Thus, the actual image ought to show the shepherd performing some service or preparing to do so. If it can be made plain in the cartoon that the help being given is relevant to the needs of the sheep, then the image has a real chance of making its point. A kneeling shepherd removing burrs from a sheep's legs would be one possibility. Even the kneeling would be a good indication of service that has nothing to do with status. Or a shepherd walking beside a sheep on its way back to the flock would do, so long as the shepherd was not pushing or prodding. The actual sheep itself, I suspect, ought to be more like a ram and less like a lamb. The shepherd ought to wear something he will not trip over while running.

A Roman Catholic priest with a soft heart for animals took pity on a baby lamb when its mother died, fed it faithfully from a bottle, and gave it tender loving care. Even though there were no other sheep around, the lamb did not seem to miss interovine relationships and got along quite well with his siblings, who were ducks. Some time later the priest went to visit a large farm, took his sheep along with him, and looked forward joyfully to introducing his friend to the sheep on the farm. He did so, but the acquaintanceship did not ripen into friendship. When he looked for his sheep, he found him down at the duck pond.

We may look further at the image of the kneeling shepherd removing burrs from the sheep. Rightly interpreted, the image should help to clarify at least the following points.

First, when the need is present, the shepherd meets it. He removes the burrs. He does not moralize to the sheep about having run off course. Whatever may have produced the predicament, he confronts and deals with it now, with tender and solicitous and, we trust, intelligent action.

Second, in order to get the sheep to stand still, he has presumably used whatever means are appropriate to secure the sheep's cooperation. Not only is the sheep respected. It is also, so to speak, consulted. The shepherd should know that next day he himself may acquire the equivalent of burrs and require help.

Third, the shepherd's kneeling shows symbolically that there are no basic or categorical differences of status, proneness to need for help, and the like, between him and the sheep. His attitude of humility manifests this fact.

Fourth, the old-style shepherding image shows, if it is rightly set forth, that our culture's movement from an agricultural to an industrial civilization need not render the metaphor irrelevant or meaningless, and that the basic needs that pastoral care tries to meet remain the same from age to age.

It is, then, both possible and necessary to make use of the old-style shepherding image. Yet we should be less than honest if we denied that it contains difficulties. The most important function of our analysis up to this point has been to rid the image of the wrong kinds of implications, and to point up sharply the two points that the image must convey: the attitude of tender and solicitous concern on the part of the shepherd and the relevance of what he is doing to the need of the sheep. We know what kinds of shepherding images may not be used. If the image we have advocated seems only partially capable of conveying the positive meanings, at least we know what those meanings are and may seek other ways of conveying them.

But there is one other possibility in the image. With the help of science and technology, literal shepherding itself has changed. A few years ago in New Zealand I had a good look at modern sheep farms. The climate there, probably like that of most of the areas described in the Bible, made it unnecessary to have buildings —unlike much sheep farming in the United States. Notable among modern methods are those which might be called "preventive." There are methods of preventing diseases, illustrated by the addition of antibiotics to the diet. There are methods of preventing loss; for example, fences not only around the property but also at the top of cliffs or other dangerous bits of terrain. There are ways of securing balanced meals through chemical analysis of the soil or purification of the water supply. Certainly these devices suggest that shepherding begins with some kind of prevention, of doing whatever can be done to prevent specific troubles from arising.

But in addition to measures of prevention I found that modern sheep farming has also made advances in the early detection of difficulties, and in a rapid approach to them once detected. The New Zealand sheep farmer who can afford it has an American Chevrolet rather than a horse, and he rides around his farm carrying binoculars. He carries a kit with him; and although he is not a veterinary physician, he has learned how to do elementary first-aid. He has also made arrangements with a veterinary physician for service as may be needed; and even small airplanes or helicopters, if they have not yet been used, are certain to come into service in the near future, whether to transport physician or sheep. If only the sheep could talk, one could even imagine walkie-talkies as a future standard installation. If we are to use this new kind of sheep farming as analogy with our own work, certainly we need to consider the walkie-talkies; for our sheep do indeed talk.

When we put together all these modern improvements in literal shepherding, we might come out with an image like this: shepherd standing beside Chevrolet, with binoculars focused on distant sheep who has caught his leg in a crevice. Or perhaps modern shepherd kneeling beside sheep with leg caught, Chevrolet in background, first-aid kit spread behind him, and binoculars temporarily laid beside first-aid kit. While there may be humorous elements about this image, it is an important reminder that the means of shepherding may change, and hopefully may improve, but that the tender and solicitous concern and the relevance of the shepherd's actions to the needs of the sheep remain constant.

The shepherding image, new style, does add a point to the shepherding image, old style. It becomes clearer that good intentions are not enough. Skill, accessibility, speed in helping, and good referral services are all shown in the new-style image in a way that the old-style cannot match. So long as the image is being used properly, then, to demonstrate the attitude and relevant action of the shepherd in relation to need, our analysis has hopefully rescued the whole business from both distortion and desuetude.

But insofar as the shepherding image seeks to show anything else, especially the attitude and action and obligation and initiative of the sheep, we must simply face the fact that it will not do. Try as we will, we cannot present sheep, however transformed, so as to manifest the proper attitudes, action, and initiative of the human being who is to seek help from his pastor. Besides, there is no use in lying or faking about sheep. They are not among the cleanest or most intelligent of animals. Their relative tractability seems to come not from goodness but from lack of imagination. In all intelligent qualities goats are far ahead of them. There is a good deal of merit in the suggestion once made to me that I write a book on *The Christian Goatherd* to match my book *The Christian Shepherd*.

Whatever merit our reconstructed shepherding image has, and we believe it to be considerable, it cannot, then, convey what needs to be interpreted about the persons who need help. Its utility is confined to the attitude of the shepherd. For an image about those needing help we must look elsewhere.

The Clinical Image

In order to convey the parishioner's side of shepherding, there seem to be four image candidates. Two of these have already been mentioned as part of our initial historical review, the doorbell image and the interview image. A third possibility is what might be called a group counseling image. And the fourth possibility is the clinical image. I plan to argue that there is some merit in each of these images, and that rightly interpreted each has a place, but that the clinical image should be central.

The clinical image shows a pastor making a bedside call upon a parishioner in hospital. The pastor should have a Bible, or a reversed collar, or a Communion kit to demonstate what he represents and to differentiate his service from that of physicians and other hospital helpers. He should be sitting on a chair beside the bed, rather than standing, partly to show that he is not administering medicine but mainly to suggest that the nature of his ministry is through conversation, talking and listening, and other procedures like prayer and reading which also involve verbal means. The parishioner is to be shown as involved in the conversation and not merely a recipient of words. His being in the hospital bed shows that he is suffering, that he is being helped by all the available means, and is thus a reminder that all available means come ultimately from God. But it shows also that, whatever the specificities of his condition, they all have a dimension that is *the* specific province of the minister of religion to help with. The parishioner is shown as accepting the minister's call in that capacity. There is no suggestion that he expects the minister to do everything he needs, nor on the other side that he expects the minister to be concerned only with narrowly religious matters and not also in his overall situation, condition, and attitude.

It may be objected that this clinical image is not normative, that a lot of the pastor's best help may be given when the parishioner is not in bed and has sufferings other than the kind that require bed. The fact is true. But our best and most convenient image of suffering is still the bed and the hospital. It should be easy enough to suggest that although the patient in bed symbolizes suffering, he does not exhaust it.

But if we retain the clinical image as central, we can then see how the counseling or interview images may be used as auxiliaries, but partially transformed from the way they originally appeared. The pastoral counseling image may show two persons, a pastor and a parishioner, seated face to face, with a cross or other symbols to show that they meet in the pastor's study or office. They meet on the same level, and face to face. Obviously there is conversation. Both should have furrowed brows or the equivalent, the parishioner to show his suffering and the pastor his concern. This image may be very important indeed, so long as it is subsidiary to the clinical image. Taken by itself, the counseling image might suggest that the pastor can do all the helping needed, or that he is concerned only with some kinds of suffering and not with all, or that this is the elite form of helping to which all others are inferior. But if this image is used as a subimage of the clinical image, then it can be very positively important.

We mentioned as another aspirant for the position of rendering the proper function of the parishioner in pastoral care a group counseling image. The merit of this would be to show that the basic helping function of ministry comes from and through the fellowship, with group attention resting, according to need, upon individual persons, under the pastor's chairmanship. The difficulties of the image are, however, very great, as it may appear to revert to the mass or flock notion. But if it can be correctly portrayed, then it, like the counseling image, could be an excellent subsidiary to the clinical image.

There is, finally, the doorbell image. For reasons that have been previously suggested, it can certainly not be the leading image. But if it is a supplementary image to the clinical image, then it can be a potent reminder that the pastor goes into the highways, byways, new housing developments, and slums to find and assist with needs, and does not merely call when needs are already known or wait until people call upon him.

I suggest, then, for shepherding an alteration of two leading images. First, in order to show the nature and quality of pastoral concern, there is the shepherding image itself, whether old style or new. Second, in order to show the place, function, and significance of the parishioner, I suggest the clinical image, with subsidiary use of the interview image, the group counseling image, and the doorbell image. All of this may appear awkward and complex. But its intent is to show the pastor as a proper shepherd and the parishioners as also doing their proper part in the helping process.

7
The Ministry as Evangelizing

Since the evangel is the good news, evangelizing is bringing that good news to those who need it and will receive it. What makes it evangelizing is not the method by which it is carried out, but the authenticity of the gospel in its relation to those who need and want it.

The fact that evangelizing cannot be defined by some particular method or methods does not mean that it can dispense with method. Like preaching and other functions of ministry, it must of course develop suitable methods and alter them according to circumstance. The great difficulty with the image of evangelizing today, however, is that it has become misjoined to a particular method and that, in reaction against this image, nothing very concrete has been put in its place.

In this discussion I shall first set forth and analyze the two dominant current images of evangelizing, and make a beginning on a third image that is emerging. I shall then use as a model or paradigm the biblical story of Jesus' sending out the twelve to preach and to heal, with some attention also to the story of he seventy. I shall then attempt a new cartoon image of evangelizing.

Current Images of Evangelizing

The dominant image of evangelizing today is the huge hall or arena, an impassioned preacher sharply spotlighted, with arms so held that they entreat the hearers to decide for Jesus Christ and then come down the aisles. Even the most sophisticated American

Christian cannot avoid thinking first of Billy Graham when evangelizing is mentioned.

Despite the fact that, at least in some respects, the Billy Graham Crusades have a sophistication unknown to Billy Sunday and the evangelizers of a previous era, the basic conception is still a residue of revivalism. And the essence of revivalism was never the size of the meeting, the number of "decisions," the folkways of the time, nor the passion of the preacher. As many of our ancestors saw clearly at the time, its essence was the conviction that methods of psychic and group pressure were both necessary and efficacious to evangelizing. Many of our forebears realized that the theological assumption involved a manipulation of the Holy Spirit. Today we also see the psychological concomitant, the "high-pressure salesmanship" that was involved in much revivalism of the nineteenth century.

Understood in this sense, "revivalism" is not properly to be associated with great evangelical leaders of the eighteenth century like Jonathan Edwards, George Whitefield, or John Wesley. Not even Whitefield tried to twist the tail of the Holy Spirit, nor did any of them count on the big meeting to do the job. It was only later on that revivalism assumed the theologically heretical pattern of which the Graham Crusades are a residue. I commend the story of the revival meeting in Mark Twain's *Huckleberry Finn*. Caricature though it is, it sees quite clearly the theological phoniness involved.

All real revivalists are too sure, too simple, and too herd-minded. Unlike Jonathan Edwards, they have not spent agonizing hours in their studies exploring what happened either in meeting or to this or that particular person. Unlike John Wesley, they have not created small groups for prayer, exchange, service, and action. Or if they have, these were gravely circumscribed—as are the Billy Graham "counseling" services, which have rigid rules in effect forbidding any natural interchange between the "counselor" and the one who has signed a card.

Some years ago I did a detailed analysis of a Billy Graham training course for "counselors." I was shocked even by some things I had not expected, such as an almost complete omission of reference to the Old Testament. I found the counselors being

113

taught to memorize the "right" scripture verse to use in replying to a question; and I found the choice of those verses severely limiting the total message even of the New Testament. Perhaps it is the Graham organization, rather than Billy Graham himself, that is accountable for such distortions. But they reveal perhaps more clearly than the Graham preaching that, even with sophistication updated, there has been no change from the nineteenth century's revivalistic attitudes that are out to make sales and are intensely suspicious of genuine human encounter.

Another way to look at revivalism is in terms of its suspicion of complexity. Is salvation in a man or a group to be wrought out through complex processes of insight and faith, doubt and backsliding, growth and regression; or does nothing count but a big moment? It takes no great imagination to see that revivalists are concerned only with what they can control. Psychologically this is unacceptable because it degrades the real complexities of personality and of interpersonal relationships. Theologically it is unacceptable because it pushes buttons and gives orders to God —always in disguised form, of course. Although this discussion is not an analysis of Billy Graham, it seems to me the time has come for churches that know better to quit taking orders from the Graham organization. If they want Graham's speaking and his charm, let them lay down the conditions and not be dictated to by the ghost of Billy Sunday.

There is also a second image of evangelizing that is widespread. This came initially from "highbrows," who realized correctly the theological heresy and narrow-mindness in revivalism, but who believed profoundly in the relevance of the Christian gospel for all men everywhere. Let us not, they said, ever be guilty of seeing evangelizing as some separate or partial function. The whole church, they added, is "mission." The whole function of the church is to be "sent" with the gospel to the needs of men. The church approximates the true Church only when its members are aware that they are church for Mission.

As a matter of fact, so far as the statement has gone, I agree wholeheartedly. But from then on, I get a little itchy both with the highbrows and the lowbrows. The highbrows, from this point onward, tend to be positivistic. Whatever they happen to be

114

interested in promoting (and usually it is very good) is defined as obedience to the "mission." But if we ask, "What have you risked lately of your personal ego in dealing with someone who does not believe in Jesus Christ as you do?" the highbrows tend to let us down. Good works of proper kinds, ecumenical engagements, discussions with captive groups of Christian laymen of all kinds—yes. But serious encounter with any agnostics less dramatic than Communists? Especially when the other fellows know their stuff! Is evangelizing to be known by its "decisions" (i.e., scalps) or by the quality of its encounters?

This conception of evangelizing as the church in mission has also, owing to the highbrows, reached a lot of the lowbrows. Occasionally the response is with great imagination and subsequent service. But all too often it is, "Gee, I'm relieved that I don't have to talk about Jesus Christ. I can just live a Christian life, go to church, make my payments, and know that the church is engaged in *mission*." The highbrows have not so intended. But in their anxiety to change the image from an offensive, "Are You Saved?" to "The Church as Mission," they have come very close to gagging the lowbrows altogether from ever saying anything to anybody about Jesus Christ—unless it is passive, pious, and programmed in advance.

The trouble with the church is mission view of evangelizing is that it welshes on the analysis of function. And because of this fact, it has no image. Nobody is *doing* anything! People are in fact doing a great deal; but if the doing is valuable, the last thing in the world one can call it is "evangelizing." If someone is healed in a missionary hospital, it is likely to be said that no effort was made to "evangelize" him. With the intent of the statement there can be no quarrel. But what a curious reversal of Christian values to assume that his being healed by a Christian institution represents something other than the gospel.

This position about evangelizing is a proper reaction against revivalism and its residues. But it has lacked the courage of its convictions, whether seen theologically or functionally. Theologically what it intends is obedience; that is, a genuine listening to the Word of God as spoken in particular situations and always from the complexities of the human psyche or of human society.

Whenever that Word breaks through, then the gospel has been heard and evangelizing is at work. Thus, a continuous critique of the methods by which we are proceeding is called for by the theology. Such a critique is not the equivalent of paying no attention to methods, especially analyzing what has not worked.

Functionally this position wants to suggest that every genuine encounter may be for or against true evangelizing, and that is correct. But to use this fact as if it implied no analysis of encounters with those who are, in various degrees, not Christian is a shirking both of the intellectual task and of the personal ambiguity of realizing that the evangelizer too must change in his attitudes.

I find it impossible to create any image for this view of evangelizing. Since it has called itself the whole function and the task, the "mission," it carries a cryptic imperialism that is not susceptible to the humble partiality of cartoons.

A third conception—and perhaps image—of evangelizing has been in process of arising for some time. Although it is, conceptually, still in rudimentary form, it has great promise. The trouble with it at the moment is that the last thing any of its agents will call it is "evangelizing."

Consider, for instance, the ministry on college and university campuses. This ministry has gone through several phases. Originally, whether at Harvard or the University of Michigan, ministry was the function of the college itself. Then with tax support, the First Amendment, fair play, and increasing heterogeneity, such ministry became "off-campus." Added to this were "chaplaincies" or "religious coordinators." Of most recent date has been the great increase, even in tax-supported institutions, of elective courses in religious subjects. It seems clear that the pattern and "mix" will have to change again in the near future.

But what chaplain, campus minister, theological teacher, or YMCA campus worker—even with the most creative program possible—would ever admit that he was out to "evangelize" students—and, above all, faculty and administration? In fact, his most creative efforts are dedicated to the encounter of the gospel with needs seen and confronted, whether personal or social. But "evangelizing"? Never! For so potent has the revivalistic image become that anything resembling the word by which it was principally known, "evangelism," is taboo. And yet some of the campus ministries are as creative in "evangelizing" as anything going today. With evangelizing, a rose by some other name seems always preferred.

Something very similar seems to be taking place in many overseas missionary projects, and indeed in some at home in areas of special need. No "decision oaths" in order to get needed service is a great fact. But do the workers giving service disassociate their service from "bringing the gospel"? Do they regard talking about the gospel as automatically impositional? I certainly want no reversions to decision oaths, which are as destructive of the real processes of coming to Christian faith as loyalty oaths are in the political realm. But who said that talk about the Christian gospel had to be impositional? Why should it not be honest, even about its doubts? Why should the evangelizer be the answer man? Can he not be the sharer of both faith and doubt?

In many missionary enterprises I see progress just as I do on university campuses. But there is a lot of what might be called "theological nonarticulation"—if you do not know the answer, say nothing. This is a travesty of Christian theology, which is not simply an answer system but is, instead, a way of connecting real life questions with fundamental and ultimate answers—which are by no means achieved or given overnight.

I have been trying to think of the image of this still nascent but emerging conception of evangelizing. The principal thing it has to suggest is dialogue. Dialogue means that, wherever you are, I am attempting to understand your situation and how you see it, . . . but also that I too stand somewhere and am not the Great Stone Face; and that, with all my attempts to be empathetic about your situation, I have the key to a treasure which, in strange and surprising ways that I cannot fathom, may help you. I have both attentiveness to you and confidence, although with humility, in my convictions. I do not push, but I reveal as seems to me relevant, right or wrong.

What kind of cartoon image can show dialogue in this sense? One possibility is an interview situation, with both persons on the same level and with one showing need not too obviously.

In a cartoon, I do not quite know how we can show that each person listens to the other seriously. If they lean forward, it may suggest that one is simply waiting to speak until the other is through. If they relax too much, it may suggest lack of concern. Perhaps they had best sit upright, but not rigid.

Perhaps our image will have to be created situationally. On a college campus, for instance, the image of evangelizing may be a round table discussion with a leader who is unapologetic but democratic. On the mission field the image might be a class that, with the guidance of its teacher, has obviously done something creative and satisfying. Or it might be a group of hospital-gowned patients in round table discussion with a doctor-leader. Perhaps we cannot achieve a universal image. But real dialogue is the intent, although not without conviction on the part of the minister.

The Twelve and the Seventy

Every time I reread the stories of the twelve and the seventy, I am reimpressed with their realism. The twelve are to take nothing along, not even a change of shirts. When people receive them, they are to stay until departure time. If they are not received, they are to shake the dust off their feet as a symbol that those cannot be helped who will not receive. They are responsible for their part in the mission, but they are not accountable for the outcome, and they are not to worry about failure if they have done their stint.

The instructions to the seventy are more detailed. They are to go two by two; and, since they are sent to places where Jesus plans later to go, they are to have his agenda in mind and not their own private program. Again the realism is evident. They are to regard themselves as lambs in the midst of wolves, not expecting everyone to fall before them. They are to take nothing and to "salute no one on the road," which seems to be a symbol of remembering their central mission against potential diversions.

When they come to a house, they are to greet its inhabitants and say, "Peace," the universal Near Eastern word of greeting.

If received hospitably, they are to stay for a time until their work is done, and not feel guilty about the free board and lodging. But they are not to be fussy about the food. They are to heal the sick and declare the presence of the Kingdom of God. Presumably, both jobs are equally the gospel.

When they are met with disdain, however, they are not to brood over it, but rather wipe the dust off their feet at the same time they declare that the Kingdom of God has come near even if the people will not believe it. They are to be sorry for such a community but not hang around it. God will have his judgment on it. Brooding is a form of judgment; so do not indulge.

When the seventy returned "with joy," they reported their astonishment that "even the demons are subject to us in your name." They had not known their own strength. At this point in the story Jesus revealed the vision that he had defeated the power of Satan and that their participation in this was only to be expected, since he had sent them out. But he concluded, "Nevertheless do not rejoice in this, that the spirits are subject to you; but rejoice that your names are written in heaven."

These two stories, in combination, seem our paradigm for evangelizing. Although the "two by two" ought not to be taken so literally as home visitation evangelism has often done, it seems symbolic of the fact that any Christian is always a representative, always more than himself, and always checked up on by his brother. He is thereby guided not to push merely his individual concerns. Perhaps, although a bit allegorically, we can suggest also that the "two by two" represents a kind of group concern and method.

Neither the twelve nor the seventy were to take anything with them. This point would seem to have two related meanings. On the one side, nothing was to get in the way of their central mission. They were not to consider homesteading. On the other side, they were to be entirely free, without vested interest except their mission to preach and to heal, in their actual encounter with the people to whom they came.

They were to bless those who received and accepted them, to get on with the preaching and healing, and to leave when their stint was finished. But if not accepted, they were to leave without brooding.

Upon their surprisedly triumphal return, the seventy were told not to be so astonished that their powers had worked. Why, indeed, were they so dumbfounded that it had happened just as Jesus said it would? Here is a useful warning that successs, even in evangelizing, always tempts away from what made the success possible.

In a schematic fashion, I think we can take the following from these stories as cardinal principles of evangelizing:

1. You are not alone when you go about evangelizing—no matter whether you are literally two by two or by yourself, or whether speaking to a group or talking to an individual or a household. You are the Lord's representative. Your brother may help you to keep this at the front of your mind.

2. While you are about the task, do not be diverted by minor things. "Salute no one on the road" if it means a diversion from your mission.

3. Your usual defense devices and resources will do you no good in this mission if you try to use them to hide behind. Make this clear to yourself by not taking an extra shirt.

4. If you are received (which does not mean that they agree with you), fine, go to work—and don't forget that both preaching and healing are your task. Do your job and get out. You are not a permanent resident.

5. If you are not received, don't be surprised. Who said everything and everybody would admire your charm and your message? Why be astonished that many people reject what could save them? It's a fact of life. Be sorry for them, but don't lose sleep over it. The judgment lies in God's hands, not in yours.

6. But when it does work, do not be surprised at that either. You have the power of the gospel whether you realize it or not. Don't get prideful when the gospel hits home through you.

7. Let your rejoicing be that your name is written in heaven— that is, that you have followed your Christian vocation, have proclaimed the gospel in both its verbal and its physical forms (preaching and healing), and that God has taken account of your stewardship.

Attitudinally speaking, I can think of nothing to add to this account of true attempts to evangelize.

A Constructive Image of Evangelizing

I propose the following as a proper image of evangelizing: a minister seated along with a group that is more than one other person but small enough to engage in discussion—and with the members of the group being quite varied as to age, sex, color, and other characteristics. The group is seated; no high pressure. They are all on the same level, but in the cartoon image the moderatorial function of the minister may properly be shown. He represents a gospel and is unapologetic about its authority.

Since we live in the kind of world we do, a good addition to the basic image would be one person seated directly beside the minister, obviously acting as a translator—since language too is a variant. The minister does not expect everybody to "speak English," nor does he resent the waiting, either way, in his communications. The translator is a reminder that the minister, whatever his resources, cannot get through to everybody by himself.

The fault of this image is that it stressses the verbal side of evangelizing and does not succeed in demonstrating also the healing which was equally important to the twelve and the seventy. The best I can do, in this single image, is to suggest that a couple of members of the group be shown with a cast on the arm or a bottle of medicine in front of them. Beyond that, our single image would have to become a filmstrip.

The other fact omitted from this image is more difficult to deal with. It is the people who will not receive you. In a filmstrip the minister could be shown shaking the dust off his shoes. But how can we show him engaged in evangelizing and yet being entirely rejected? For it must be remembered that evangelizing is intelligent effort, and not necessarily success. We must simply keep in mind that our basic image fails to show this fact.

Despite its inevitable limitations, this image seems thoroughly faithful to the New Testament paradigms. Provided the image is genuine, and not something trumped up for the cartoonist, we may assume that the following things are true in the background:

1. On the part of the minister there is an empathetic or phenomenological concern for the attitudes of all the other people (and their conditions such as broken arms) to all serious things, including Christian faith but not confined to it, regardless of the existing content of those views and conditions. Judgment in a pro or con sense is suspended in favor of testimony through understanding, and that is the process taking place. The minister has full confidence in the treasure that has been accorded him. He knows it gains when he shares it. It is not a scarcity product. But if he gives it at all, he wants the real thing to be received, and not just some superficial imitation. Since he believes in it, he need not be a high-pressure salesman.

2. On the part of the group and its individual members there is great variety in several respects; but all have "received" the minister, i.e., are engaged in dialogue with him. Since they are still here, they know that they are seated on the same level as he, that they may speak honestly and do not have to follow a party line, and that he is attentive to them individually as well as in the group.

3. On the part of the whole relationship between minister and group it is clear that the movement is dynamic (energetic and in conflict), and is not wholly predictable in advance. What happens depends on the interaction, and not upon the prior attitudes of either minister or group. If negative feelings do not emerge, then there has been some secretly repressive mechanism at work. But if the interaction is open, then even the negative feelings should be received, and that reception contribute to the deepening of the relationship and thus to the chances that the gospel will be given and received.

In our own day virtually all evangelizing must be done in a "boundary" situation or it is not done at all. Finding candidates for the gospel who have never heard the name of Jesus Christ, but who are so ready for the whole Christian message that they simply fall at our feet—this never happens. Instead, we have the logical skeptic, or the one whom the evil in the world has embittered, or he who has given up serious things since life is a joke, or she who is dogmatic about something else. And many others. For none of them is "receiving" us likely to mean, "Give me the truth, brother, and I will accept it without question." It is, instead, the readiness to enter into dialogue. And a very large number are ready to do so if our attitude makes sense.

For a time "Christian apologetics" went out of fashion. Perhaps this was due in part to the debased meaning of apology as excuse rather than its proper sense of confident explanation. More of it, however, was due to the Continental emphasis on "proclamation," with the implication that "apologetics" is always trying to compromise the truth. I believe any such allegation to be a misunderstanding of the issue. There is no contradiction between one's best and most confident grasp of the Word and his equal attentiveness to the attitude of the person with whom he is in conversation. If one's interpretation of the Word cannot abide questioning, then it is defensive and not confident. If it is eroded by a breath of doubt from another, then it was not genuine to begin with.

There is another fact of our present cultural situation that bears heavily upon the image of evangelizing that has been presented. This is our Western, and especially American, suspicion of words without deeds. What the gospel is, is what it does. Surely one must approve the rising interest in appropriate Christian social action in all its relevant forms. But beneath this there is sometimes an improper suspicion of anything but action, even a suspicion that service disappears if analyzed. Some of this is a by-product of anti-intellectualism, but more of it comes from a kind of idealism. Recently the great Czechoslovakian Protestant theologian, Josef Hromádka, was quoted as saying that the Iron Curtain countries are realizing that there is a problem of man and not just of social organization. Learning the same lesson is not much easier in the West, even for Christians. Action is needed indeed. But there need be no shamefacedness for concentrating at the point where man in conflict may finally come to see the light. That is the proper business of evangelizing.

Evangelistic Conversation

These samples are put in the form of one-to-one conversations. But the principles would seem to be the same in face-to-face groups and, with the minister mentally supplying the other side of the dialogue, in preaching and other large group presentations.

First Conversation

Mr. McCall: I know you ministers must be disturbed by these so-called "radical theologians" saying that God is dead or that we only need Jesus. But, you know, Paul van Buren has struck a chord with me. I've been skeptical for a long time about your whole series of Christian claims. Van Buren tells me that I may be right.

Pastor Green: I take it, then, that, in a backhanded way, van Buren has got you interested in theology?

Mr. McCall: I guess that's right. I simply paid no attention to it before. Now I think it is important at least to take a look. Otherwise, I shouldn't have bothered to attend that lecture by Bishop Robinson in your church last week.

Pastor Green: I take you as an honest inquirer, Mr. McCall. Obviously, I believe in God and am willing to tell why. Also, I think Paul van Buren makes some very important points. But I think what interests me most is why it took a statement that was apparently radical and negative to get you going on this interest. How about that?

Second Conversation

Mr. Carnahan: It happened just before five o'clock, pastor. Apparently he was turning when the truck came along and hit him. The neighbors called Mary, and the ambulance; and fortunately nobody touched him until the ambulance came.

Mrs. Carnahan: It was ghastly. He had blood on his face (*she cries*).

Mr. Carnahan: When we saw the surgeon, just an hour ago, he had made his examination. And (*he clenches fists and breathes heavily*) we seem to face an impossible situation (*he pauses*).

Pastor Brown: What has happened is a terrible thing. Do I gather from what you say that Joe's life is in danger?

Mr. Carnahan: Pastor, it's even worse than that. Dr. McMurdo says that Joe's brain is so injured that his chance of living would be increased if the tissues were removed. But if this is done, then, he says, Joe is less likely to be a "full human being," as he put it. He recommends that we do not operate.

Pastor Brown: That's an intensely difficult decision. And I gather the doctor has asked you to make it?

Mrs. Carnahan: Yes, and he says that if there is to be an operation, it must be no later than tomorrow morning. Oh, pastor, what shall we do?

Mr. Carnahan: What does God say in a situation like this, if he says anything at all?

Third Conversation

Mrs. Stroback: If it had been the Second World War, I think I might have stood it. But Vietnam—and he was only twenty-three.

Pastor Black: That is, it isn't so much your questioning your son's death in the war, but rather that this particular war is so hard to understand?

Mrs. Stroback: Oh, yes. So many brilliant people say we shouldn't be there at all, and that even if we win, we will lose. But it was *my* son who was killed there.

Pastor Black: If you felt that John had really contributed to the future of our world, the burden would be less. But, as it is . . .

Fourth Conversation

Joe: Oh, so you're a minister. Slumming down here in our section; are you?

Pastor White: I'm interested in getting acquainted with some of you.

Joe: Sociological study, huh?

Pastor White: In a way, yes. I am puzzled by what many of you hope to get from this kind of life.

Joe: I'll tell you one thing. I'm sure as hell not going back to those damned suburbs. Everything is tight and clean and well-knit—on the surface. And beneath it, the whole damn place is a seething sink. Whatever it means, I want honesty.

Pastor White: There *is* a lot of hypocrisy in American life, especially the suburbs. I gather you feel that living down here at least avoids that?

Fifth Conversation

Mike Dumas: Gee, I'm sorry, reverend, I wouldn't have swore if I'd knowed you was a reverend. But you hadn't ought to've had the hind end of your car so close to my truck.

Pastor Blue: We've been over that and that and I agree that I shouldn't. But you had your own mind on something else too, you know.

Mike Dumas: Yeah, guess I did, reverend. But anyhow, I'm sorry I cussed.

Pastor Blue: I've heard cussing before, and I suspect the Lord has too. But I gather it does bother you a bit that you let loose before a minister?

In precisely such boundary circumstances as these does the minister decide as to whether he is evangelizing—successfully or otherwise is not his responsibility—and all consistent with his obligations of pastoral care, social action, self-protection, and the like. If he cannot do it in situations of this kind, he is faking it in the pulpit or arena.

Methods of Evangelizing

I have already given away my own conviction about methods of evangelizing; namely, that methods relate more to attitudes than to techniques. Whether in private conversation, group discussion, a sermon or a speech, or in the interaction within the community, the question is whether there is, on the one side, conviction about what the gospel means and, on the other side, unqualified readiness to hear the other people and see the world from their point of view. Without the attitude, no method in the sense of technique will accomplish much. At the same time, if there is the attitude, then discriminating attentiveness to method is useful.

The minister can and must of course help his lay men and women to see that they too are engaged in evangelizing. I agree with all the literature declaring the importance of this ministry of the laity to the world. There are two troubles with it. One is that a lot of conscientious laymen feel guilty when they don't have the name "Jesus Christ" on their lips, and their teachers have not helped them to understand any better. The other is that many evangelizing contacts, just like pastoral contacts, need understanding at a professional level; and no ordained minister should get rid of his obligation for them on the ground that ministry is by all Christians. Helping many people to understand the gospel treasure is no more a business for tyros than is delicate pastoral care under pain and suffering.

As the constructive image suggests, my first focus of method lies in small group discussion. The image shows a great variety of people. Some of these may already be related to the church, so that meetings may be in the church buildings—whether conducted by the minister or by someone else. But if the variety is to be real and not overly limited, then the minister must get out from the apse and the nave and meet the small groups where he can —no matter what the starting subject. Once he gets a group, from there on he is on his own—hopefully with God's help.

Pastoral contacts of all kinds, as suggested in the sample conversation snatches, are of very great importance. Even "routine calls" may be valuable if seen from this perspective. Many pastoral calls have evangelizing overtones if the minister is alert to them. And how do you handle that likable atheist at the Rotary Club?

The big question about evangelizing is: What kind of special events? I see nothing wrong with special events as such. The question is the attitude toward them, how they are conducted, and how people are taught to participate in leadership. I am partial to home visitation by teams of lay people, and have written somewhat about this. But I know quite well that the difference between a fake campaign and a vital ministry lies in the special education of the callers beforehand. Most ministers seem to despair of teaching their laymen "how," and consequently resort to exhortation and aphorisms. The results are usually poor. My impression is that ministers who get over their own reluctance about talking "how" with their lay calling training groups get excellent results.

There is a special realism about home visitation by lay teams in American culture. More than half our people, at least nominally, are church-related; and another big swatch think kindly toward the churches even if they do not belong. So long as there is no high pressure, few Americans regard a call from church representatives as invasion. Further, with all our groups and groupiness, we Americans are a lonely people. A fifth of us move our homes every year. We always feel a bit uncertain—despite our loud protestations to the contrary—that we belong. The first thing I would say to a group of home visitation callers is: If you don't really want these people—whatever their color, national origin, and so on—then quit right now. On the fundamentals, you can't

127

fake. Why leave all the racial education to social action? Why not get evangelizing into the act as it should be?

As to special speakings, sermons, large group discussions, and so on, my general observation is that these are successful according to the degree: (1) that they are competently planned; (2) that they fit both fore and aft into the ongoing life of the organization, be it local church, college, hospital, or some other institution. I have long since discarded the prejudice that a lecture—especially followed by discussion—can accomplish nothing. The question is whether the special events respect the processes of human development and decision, or seek shortcuts through the residues of revivalism.

I have been fascinated by the number of secular institutions in these last years (often mental hospitals) who have asked me to do what would have been called in a previous period "religious emphasis week." To be sure, they would not have tolerated direct-down-the-sawdust altar calls. But so long as I did engage in perfectly honest discussion on the issues raised, I have found myself astonishingly free to be as Christian and as theological as I could. I doubt that any other nation has so many secular organizations with such openness to honest discussion from a Christian point of view—so long as it is informed, fair-minded, and of some interest. This seems to me our greatest evangelizing opportunity today. Perhaps, as a seminary professor, I am in a special position to be drawn into it. I often get the impression, however, that many ministers overlook precisely these golden opportunities in their own front yards.

Speaking of evangelistic methods, I should mention many other avenues, like the arts, the humanities, and the social sciences. In an increasingly secularized culture it always astonishes many people that Christian faith and Christian churches should believe in the arts, the humanities, and the sciences. Let us have no morality plays that tell how much one's income is increased if he is a Christian. But on all other legitimate levels, just having these interests going in intelligent hands is itself an excellent method of evangelizing, of telling the gospel story to all sorts and conditions of men.

The Uneasiness of Evangelizing

I decided once that I could make up a testing instrument on the basis of asking ordained and lay Christians, "What do you think about evangelizing?" My guess was that the results would tell me a great deal more about the respondent's personality, degree of organization-mindedness, vision and imagination, theology, and general good sense than he would realize when answering my question. Let me give some hypothetical samples to my hypothetically posed question.

1. *"Why of course we do it through our Christian education program."* I am all for Christian education. But unless this is an exceptional respondent, what he means is that his church is going about business as usual with no attentiveness to the boundary situations which may also occur with children.

2. *"Our church is for it. We have a special week every year."* No comment is needed. Whatever the merit of the special week, the obvious fact is that it is a concession and not built in, fore and aft, to the total program of the church.

3. *"We call on all new prospects."* A good thing to do, to be sure, but somewhat lacking in New Testament enthusiasm.

4. *"Evangelism? That Graham stuff? Our church is working for racial justice."* A very good thing too. But the message of Jesus Christ is for all men regardless of color.

5. *"We are exchanging this and that with a group over in the South End; and this has won us some people and lost others."* Great program, results ambiguous—as to be expected with anything creative. But is this a substitute for evangelizing here, or in the South End?

6. *"Our emphasis is on making the gospel more real to our own people."* Great stuff, if it can be managed. But no church that focused solely within has ever made if for long. Are you afraid to talk to anybody who does not agree with you?

7. *"Evangelism? We think that's old hat. We think the church itself is mission! And laymen are the heart of the mission. Come to our hamburger roast for hippies next Friday evening at Hollywood and Vine."* Unhappily, the hippies will only drop in to get the free goodies.

129

To be sure, there is a reasonable facsimile of caricature in the above samples; but I think they ring a bell here and there.

So massive has been the revivalist image of evangelizing (and its residues) that anybody with any sophistication tends to duck the whole business. This seems to me a grave error. For evangelizing, in its essence, is taking the authentic Christian gospel (albeit with the limitations of human understanding) through word or deed to those who need it and are at least prepared enough to take a look at it.

We have a great deal of creative evangelizing today—all under some other name. So long as we do not impede the creative activity, let us get our labels straight.

But we also have a lot of pussyfooting about Christian talk. Either—with all your quite human and legitimate and God-understood doubts—you think we have something, or you don't. If you can't talk at all unless you are too sure to be sensible, then by all means keep silent, to the benefit of everybody. But if, with more insight into your human ambiguity, which we all share, you nevertheless have some kind of Christian faith—then, as appropriate to the situation, how about getting it into the encounter?

It seems to me high time that we got evangelizing out of the theological basement. If we have a treasure to be shared with all men who will receive it (not without some intermediary discussion), then let us get on with it; and not refuse to call our most imaginative efforts by their right name.

8
The Ministry as Celebrating

In Protestantism the central image of celebrating is quite clear. It shows minister standing or sitting at a Communion table, with laymen by his side. The standing or sitting is mostly a matter of which part of the service is being depicted. Clearly, the Communion service, by any of its names—the Eucharist, the Lord's Supper or Table, the Communion Service, the Sacrament of the Altar, or simply the Sacrament—is the paradigm and center of all Christian celebrating.

The Lord's Supper

In traditional Protestantism three facts have been crucially important about the central image of celebrating. The first has been the presence of a table with the elements upon it. The table represented the meal together that Jesus had had with his disciples in the upper room. The table was not to be construed as an altar in any sense that would imply this service as offering a necessary sacrifice. Whether Protestants were right or wrong in so interpreting the Roman Catholic Mass is of course another question.

The second fact about the image has been the leadership of the minister in the events of the celebration—". . . as I ministering in his name." Even though wide sections of Protestantism balked on the word "priest," this phrase is as clear a functional conception of priesthood as one could have. No less than in the Catholic Mass, Protestantism required a set-aside minister, by whatever name, to be the principal celebrant.

131

The third historically important fact about the image is the presence of the laymen. Ordinarily they are "special" laymen, in some churches ordained as elders. They are responsible representatives of the people, just as the ordained minister is supposedly a responsible representative of Jesus Christ. The minister cannot do all the things himself that the service requires. Nor does he merely need technical assistants such as altar boys. Although functionally different roles are assigned, those of the laymen are just as important as that of the ordained minister.

So far as these three crucial elements of the image are seen in terms of what they stand for positively, I see no reason for dissent from the wisdom of our forefathers. They emphasized the table as the fellowship and the communal celebrating. They stressed equally the leadership of the ordained minister and the necessary and responsible participation in that leadership by laymen.

In the background, however, they were frying some polemical fish which, over the centuries, have acquired a bad odor even if not entirely rotten. The most obvious polemic was against sacrifice, altar, and priest. Yet the historical fact is that the Last Supper was set within the context of the Passion as a whole, and at the Supper Jesus looked ahead to the approaching crucifixion. Perhaps Protestants were correct in being against some aspects of the ingenuity with which the Catholic Mass had woven these strands together. But in having no element at all of "altar," they narrowed the context in which the total celebration must be seen and understood. The creation of the term "Sacrament of the Altar" in modern Lutheranism seems a clear and important way of moving beyond the polemics of an earlier time.

Something similar is involved in the aversion to having the ordained minister known as a "priest." My etymological pony explains that most words for "priest" go back to a word for "elder," while others derive from a child's word for "father." In etymological honesty, it must also be admitted that other words eventually led to "king" or "prince" or "lord"—terms involving authority over rather than wisdom or honor or representativeness. And of course it was this authoritarian connotation of "priest" to which early Protestants objected.

With the concept of the universal priesthood of believers, they

132

almost had it. The boldness of this notion is that it makes priest-hood a function and not a status. Had they been wholly consistent, they would have called the ordained minister at a celebration of the Lord's Supper a "priest" without batting an eye; for he is there performing a function, with assistance. But so great was the fear that doing so would have status implications that it was seldom done in Protestantism except in the Church of England.

Some injustice was also done to "sacrifice." On the positive side, it was good to show that the sacrifice by Jesus Christ was all sufficient for all time. But the grave Protestant suspicion of any kind of theology of works or merit made it difficult for people to participate emotionally and empathetically in the great sacrificial event. The Protestant suspicion about celebrating Good Friday is both a demonstration of this suspicion and a result of it. Psychologically speaking, Catholic practice has been much wiser.

An effective way of retaining our Protestant positive insights about the central celebrating image, and yet to move beyond the "smoke-filled room" aspects that became involved with them, is to take a look at the several terms for this central act of celebrating.

The Communion service emphasizes fellowship and relatedness. It also means "sharing in." But fellowship is either reconciling or it is not fellowship at all. That is, if there were no barriers to positive communality, no service would be needed. Just as did the disciples at the Last Supper, so Christians in all ages bring enmity, strife, party spirit, bitterness, indifference, and hypocrisy to the Communion today. There should be no need to apologize for the fact that things are so bad, within the conflicted psyche of the person and in the interpersonal and group relationships, that the "medicine" of Communion is needed. In the Communion service, the Kingdom begins now.

How does our central image look in the light of Communion? Generally speaking, it looks good. There is the fellowship table, the representativeness of the leader, and the clear and responsible participation by other leaders on behalf of the people. But it does not show that both Judas and Peter are present, the one who is to betray and the other, temporarily, to deny. The danger is that the Communion interpretation of the sacrament will be seen as a fellowship-fixer, rather than just what it was in the instance of the Last Supper, containing and accepting ambiguity.

The Lord's Supper, or the Lord's Table, emphasizes that we are being fed. We are being fed with ordinary human food (not a balanced diet, it must be admitted), because we are organic creatures and we need it. But this food was likened by Jesus at the Last Supper to his body and his blood. By his express command we are, as were his disciples, to be symbolically "God-eaters." We are to incorporate—make part of our bodies—the flesh and the blood that he was about to give up at the time of the Last Supper. And we are to have no guilt feelings about this theophagy, i.e., God-eating. It is, to be sure, symbolic. But it should remind us, while at the same time it relieves us, of our perpetual human aggressive and "incorporating" drives, just as the very acts of eating and drinking remind us of our animal and organic nature. We commemorate *his* Last Supper. In this act we are renewed, and also reminded humbly of our human condition.

How does the central image emerge in light of the Lord's Supper? The answer is: Pretty well, except that everything has tended to become too neat. The elements, with all those people to feed, look so small that they are unlikely to support anybody even until he gets home for Sunday dinner. And the fact that something of symbolic sacredness is to be incorporated is not wholly clear in the image. We might go off from the service either still feeling guilty or without a new humility about our condition. No image, of course, can do everything. But our central image tends to play down the "body and blood." To be sure, literal body and blood were not present at the Last Supper. Since Jesus himself represented them symbolically, we can do so too. It might help a good deal if we had some real bread and some real wine, and not wafers and grape juice.

The Eucharist puts stress upon thanksgiving and gratitude. True and sustained gratitude, however, is one of the rarest of human feelings. Oscar Wilde caught this very well when he pointed to a certain man and said he did not know why the other was so angry because he, Wilde, had never done anything for him. One cannot feel thanks without having acknowledged the need and the weakness that were met by the act of graciousness. So there is no unadulteratedly pure gratitude. The Eucharist knows all this. It leads to a capacity for genuine thanksgiving, and does not require it as an admission ticket.

Does our central image know it too? Perhaps it does, but the image itself does not make it manifest. The people around the table all look as if they were too well adjusted, including the minister. Perhaps the minister could be shown with a lock of hair out of place, and maybe one lay member could look a bit like a hippie. If, in some symbolic way, a bit of ambivalence could be shown about gratitude, the resulting image would be more true to the actual situation.

The Sacrament of the Altar, or the service seen as the Mass, emphasizes the Lamb of God, the perfect and wholly adequate atoning sacrifice, whose goodness and whose acts blot out the sin of mankind. Since this is so, no further sacrifice by men is needed. But men do need to feel participatively with the enormity and the anguish of the sacrifice. The everyday pathology of sacrifice is that a person "gives up" something and then feels so righteous as a result that his demands become outrageous. His act of sacrifice is a kind of button-pushing device for special favors. The Sacrament of the Altar does not so much repress this human tendency as channel and relocate it. It becomes transformed.

At this point, perhaps above all others, our central image is clearly weak. It contains no hint of participation in sacrifice except in the form of the very symbolic elements. Really red wine that looks like blood and very rough bread that resembles flesh might help. Or it could be that, at the moment the image is snapped, all the participants, even though round the table, could be on their knees. What is needed is the sense of participation in the sacrifice that has been made, and not the smug sense that "that is all over with," although in a sense it is.

There is finally "the Sacrament" in Protestant language, even though baptism is yet another sacrament. The emphasis in this usage has been upon the "sign" or "seal" function, tamping down in human hearts what God has already made known through his Word. Here the worshiper is encouraged to receive and participate

135

at a level deeper than his conscious reasoning; but at the same time he becomes motivated to reflect subsequently upon a better understanding of the Word in the light of his experience of the Sacrament. His obtuseness, defensiveness, and narrow-mindedness are not rejected, but they are in part transformed.

Our central image has nothing to say against this interpretation, and something for it in the form of the visible symbols of bread, wine, and table. But it is not very explicit. How can there be pictorial representation of the closed-mindedness to which the Sacrament addresses itself?

In these considerations of the principal ways in which the sacramental acts shown in the central image are represented, I have tried to show the multidimensional perspective that must be taken in order to grasp the meaning of each and all. The central image comes through pretty well. But it seems clear that it must be supplemented and that it can be made more adequate through a few details like red wine, rough bread, some persons who are less than sartorially perfect, and not unambivalent bliss on the face of the minister.

The Human Function of Celebrating

One of the perils of civilization is that celebrating may be put on a purely private basis for routine use (with a sophisticated denial that it is "solemnizing"), or else it may become *ad hoc* improvisation in its public character. The latter was well illustrated at the time of President John F. Kennedy's death. The television and radio newscasters thought, before, that they were merely reporters and commentators. During the critical two or three days they found that they had to become also priests of a kind. Most of them were not up to it. Fortunately, the Roman Catholic funeral service on Monday morning finally appeared to offer some stability and continuity against the well-intentioned but unrehearsed priestly rituals of the preceding days.

The privatizing of celebrating is well demonstrated by the strong shift in privatism about funerals during the past generation. A competent student of mine studied this change in a small but long-established town near Princeton. He found that, even a generation ago, the whole community was involved in several ways when a death took place. Today the death and funeral he found to be strictly a matter of the family, with technical and temporary assistance afforded by the church and the undertaker. Even in the death of persons who have made unusual contributions to society, the family tends to be left alone with its grief except for the funeral or memorial service.

These drifts of the sophisticated toward privatism and opportunism in celebrating may of course contain positive potentialities. People who do not want to be intruded on in time of grief, for instance, may be better protected. A newly married couple may celebrate in their own way and not in that dictated by friends or custom. And the "opportunism" may, for example in worship, be creative, and elaborate the means while being faithfully attentive to the ends. I am not unduly pessimistic about the longer future in these matters. But right now I think celebrating is in bad odor, and this does no good to anybody.

If the mythical observer from Mars were briefed on the concept of celebrating, and then permitted to take his flying saucer to various celebrative events, I believe he might say something like the following concerning what his observations told him about the human race.

1. These are a self-transcendent people. Whether they like it or not, they can do proper forgetting and proper remembering only through celebration. By the same token, they can look ahead only if they celebrate as well as plan.

2. These are a people of feeling. To them, not every event is the same. Some are big and important and must be celebrated—whether through joy or sorrow. Others are small and can be handled privately. The bigger the feeling, the greater the need for celebrating.

3. These are a people trying to combine creative novelty with tradition. Every important celebration contains at least a bit of novelty. But heavy reliance is placed on the celebrations of tradition. Thus, these people believe in continuity and stability; but they are innovators as well.

4. These people use celebrations as a way of obeying but also going beyond the law. They are not lawless although even the

137

most responsible of them takes pride in rejecting a law in which he does not believe. Many celebrations enable them to be for the law but above it, even if the "above" is only temporary.

5. These are a "totemic" people. They have an immense number of taboos, some of which are sensible and some not. But whether through special occasions, like Mardi Gras, or repeated events, like the Mass, they try symbolically to combine the sense of social responsibility represented by taboo with the creative and spontaneous yen toward something beyond.

6. The best celebrations are an extraordinary combination of freedom and restraint. When they are very good, nobody violates the important restraints. When they become eroded, a lot of the participants do not know the difference.

7. Perhaps above all, the celebrations show that human beings are aware of living in both darkness and light. For human well-being, these must be constantly distinguished—even though they are not always apparent to the outside observer.

Our mythical friend from Mars, in his preceding comments, has not so much characterized human celebrations (for they are more varied than he had opportunity to see) as he has said what the fact of human celebrating tells about human beings.

In human evolution the civilizing and moralizing of celebrations was a triumph all the way. We are indeed the kind of people noted by the mythical Martian. But if it were not for the institutions of religion, as we now call them, celebrating anything solemnly and seriously might well be left to privacy or public adventitiousness. I rather think that man from Mars thought celebrating a good thing.

Celebrating Through Ritual

Whatever else ritual may suggest, it means that you do it more than once. Ritual is common agreement about sequence. Ritual is the acknowledgment of chronology. Whether we are celebrating the Lord's Supper, Christmas, a marriage, or a funeral, ritual tells us in a kindly way that all this has happened before, although it does not need to deny the uniqueness of what is happening now.

Ritual (the same procedures have been used before) both reveals and conceals. That is, it reveals what is going on at various levels, and the participant may enter and understand at these various levels. But any good ritual refrains from clobbering the participant. If he is not prepared to accept deeper levels, he is not penalized thereby. So far as I can see, nobody at any time gets every level of something so celebrative as the Communion service. Even the minds of the greatest Christians have wandered when such and such was mentioned. But ritual is not a clobberer. Even the saint may get it next week or next day. Only out of a climate of familiarity can novelty and insight and true critical acumen develop. To regard ritual, therefore, as only revealing, and not also as concealing, would be false to the facts and an impediment to the growth of Christian vision.

Just as ritual both reveals and conceals in relation to meaning, so it both opens up and protects in regard to feeling. Both during the ritual and in subsequent reflection, this or that phrase may jump out at us as describing either our particular situation or the situation of human beings in general—whether it be "miserable sinners," or "no health," or something else. In the same way, the nature of God as described in vivid phrases of the ritual may hit us at some time—"merciful," for instance. The relation between ourselves and God may also come into highlighted status through our reflection at some point in the ritual. For instance, "while we were sinners," God did such and such. It may strike home. Especially because we are still as much sinners as ever. But God made allowance.

One may of course argue that, in these instances of insight and new positive reflection, it is not ritual but something else— like the Word—that has come through. But how could there be the "build-up," the preparation, and indeed the whole climate and context to make possible both questions and answers, without the repetition of ritual? How can you tell if your new shoes really fit— until a couple of days later?

Ritual is both like common life and unlike it. The modern liturgical movement, Catholic and Protestant, has made the point clearly that ritual and liturgy are not removed from the actual events and decisions and emotions of life, but are representations of precisely those realities. This is very true. Gregory Dix's analysis of worship through the Mass shows it to be related to actual living at every phase. Even a so-so service of Protestant worship begins with a combination of confession and thanksgiving, proceeds through the Word as guiding and sustaining us, commands our response in the offertory and dedication, and lets us go in peace but not without problems. Thus, Christian worship of any kind is related to life's actual events and decisions.

But if the creative liturgists will forgive me, liturgy is not life itself. Liturgy is remembrance, recollection, and anticipation. It is typological life. It is "controlled" life. Not all living is controlled. Thus, liturgy is a representation of what life, with all its conflicts and decisions, is. But actual concrete life often seems otherwise, not only as to the decisions but also as to recognizing when a decision should be made.

In 1907 Sigmund Freud published an important paper comparing and contrasting the psychic dynamisms he had discovered in dealing with obsessional neuroses and what seemed to him the underlying situation in religious rituals. His paper was descriptive. He did not allege that religious rituals were neurotic. But he found three features that the two kinds of phenomena seemed to have in common.

First, he saw an extraordinary conscientiousness in the performance of the acts. Second, he saw severe pangs of conscience if anything were, however inadvertently, omitted. Third, he saw the ritualistic acts, like the obsessive acts, as being carried on somehow apart from the world of the ordinary—for instance, in buildings of a different type.

There is great insight in Freud's analysis. It is indeed true that obsessive rituals of the type Freud examined in the individual are carried out without awareness of the deeper forces in his personal history that he is holding at bay through his actions. Insofar as a religious ritual has lost contact with the dynamic forces that brought it into being, it does precisely take on the features noted by Freud. And who could deny the extent to which this is true?

The one way in which a religious group can avoid falling into this trap is to be constant and fearless in its analysis—historical, psychological, and otherwise, as well as theological—about its own ritual, and always bringing multidimensional perspectives to bear.

Religious rituals that are authentic bring together in solemn manner many levels of human psychic functioning: aspiration, aggression, gratitude, appeasement, and many others. But as time goes on, they tend to become neat and pretty, and then have a much more difficult time making contact with the several levels of psychic life.

Finally, although our precise knowledge is still small, we now know in a general way that different persons are affected differently by religious rituals. The difference applies not only to types of rituals but also to ritual in itself. Whatever might be the merit on theological grounds, therefore, a single massive form of ritual across Christendom would be likely to lose a lot of customers. Legitimate variation as well as creative novelty seem just as important as awareness of the roots.

Types of Christian Celebrating

The first type is that shown in the central image of the Lord's Supper. Here the celebrating is regular and rather frequent, and intended for all adults. In the Roman Catholic Church confession is supposedly on the same general basis—for all adults and relatively frequent. Some groups in Christian history used foot-washing in a similar way. And of course in Protestantism there are always "services of worship" of all kinds, as indeed there are in Catholic practice too.

The second type of celebration focuses on one person at one time; and he at that proper time is the focus of the celebrating— although ordinarily a congregation will be present. This is of the general nature of baptism, of confirmation or joining the church, of either marriage or ordination, whichever is chosen, and in the Roman Catholic Church of extreme unction.

A third type of celebration also focuses upon the person, but the acts are performed according to his need and may be repeated under proper conditions. The anointing carried out for healing by the Church of the Brethren is an illustration of this, as are the bedside prayers of the pastor in the hospital. On an informal basis in Protestantism, except for a few wings of Anglicanism and Lutheranism, hearing a confession is of this type. Especially in connection with illness, there is an increasing tendency to bring the Mass or the Lord's Supper to the person according to his special need. And in those segments of Protestantism in which remarriage after divorce is approved under conditions, then marriage falls into this group.

The fourth type of celebrating is on an annual basis and is ordinarily guided by the church year—at least to the extent of focusing on Advent and Lent, even if Pentecost is often forgotten. And finally there are the great special events and congresses of all kinds, including ecumenical types of celebration.

Perhaps it should be noted, since it is in such vivid contrast to Judaism, that one type of religious celebrating is conspicuously absent from the Christian list. That is holding major religious acts in the home, as do the Jews. The Christmas tree and the Easter bunny may have their points, but they are not solemnizations as are the Jewish home festivals.

What is the point of this typology? It is simply to suggest that, despite the basic adequacy of our central Christian image of celebrating, corollary images will need to be used if the whole network of celebrating is to hang together.

Celebrating and Living

Throughout this discussion it has been argued, in line with the central point of the liturgical movement, that religious celebration is closely related to actual life itself with its conflicts, its variety, its joys, and its sorrows. Religious celebrating that becomes so "apart" that it has lost the connections is simply going through obsessional motions. Live religious ritual is proper adaptation to the deeper things of living.

But celebrating is only a part of actual living even though it solemnizes, honors, praises, commemorates, observes, and is repentant about everything in life that has ultimate meaning and significance. Celebrating, while related to life, is no substitute for living.

Since ministers too have different kinds of responses to celebrating—and to different types of celebrating—they are always in danger of allowing personal preference or antipathy to determine the attention given to their leadership in celebrating. With the relative freedom given to Protestant ministers, it is possible to make so much, or so little, of celebrating that people are either surfeited or short-changed.

It may be argued that in Protestantism there is some check on these tendencies because a minister has to conduct at least one celebration a week; and if his robes become too colorful and dazzling, the committee will speak to him. While there is some truth in this, I find myself equally suspicious of the minister whose delight is in every pew and picture that he personally installed, and of him who uses celebrations only as "the preliminaries" for what he is going to preach.

And so I feel that our central Protestant image of celebrating—minister at table holding the elements, and lay associate leaders by his side—is properly the paradigm of all Christian celebrating. It does, however, need constant rethinking and reinterpretation lest the historically polemic elements it originally implied should make it weak or partly irrelevant. We need additional images of celebrating—in joy as in sorrow, annually as well as weekly—to aid the central image.

9
The Ministry as Reconciling

In no other age has it been so clear that the ministry must be engaged in the processes of reconciling. Whether we begin with married couples, parents and children, people of different races, nations, or the relations among people of different religious faiths, we realize that the quantities of the unreconciled exceed anything ever before known in human history. Ordained Christian ministers may of course have only a small role to play in the gigantic tasks of reconciling that confront us. But unless we play that part, we may not get a chance at performing creatively the other functions of ministry.

Reconciling may mean either "bring into harmony" or "render no longer opposed." There is a very important and subtle difference between these two shades of meaning. I may have my arms around you, or I may only have agreed to discard my weapons. It is high time that reconciling be desentimentalized sufficiently to recognize that the second meaning is often relevant, important, and the best that can be hoped for in the situation.

We have no indigenous Christian image of the ministry as reconciling. Part of the reason for this fact is that "reconciling" (along with salvation and similar terms) has been used in theology to refer to the work of Jesus Christ; and since his work has been all sufficient in its foundational principle, it has not seemed appropriate to present an image of human-level reconciling except derivatively through Jesus Christ. And since the processes of establishing reconciliation once for all, and of nurturing the outworking of it in particular situations, are not the same, the image becomes elusive.

144

All the functional images of ministry deal with what we do. The context of each image, and its elements, are supplied Christologically. But the actuality of human action and ministry is not simply a mirror image of the life of Jesus even as the Christ. In this instance, in the absence of any clear historical precedent, we shall have to think of possible candidates for the reconciling image of ministry, drawing as needed upon secular sources.

Possible Images of Reconciling

The traditional general image of reconciliation is the handshake. And the church has often used "the right hand of fellowship." Originally this symbol was a demonstration that the hand-offerer was not carrying a weapon. Hence it involved the long approach before hands ever actually met. It was alert about threat. But the long approach showing a weaponless hand, and then the grip, were symbols that at least for the time being the threat had been set aside.

If the handshake retained its original meaning—being honest about the hostility and being attentive visually to the long approach and not merely the clasp—it might be a candidate for a reconciling image. For whatever else reconciling may require, it must have an acknowledgment of grievances and a long approach. Today a handshake is merely a form of greeting among acquaintances, less intimate than the kiss or caress but more personal than the nod or bow. Furthermore, in the churches the right hand of fellowship does not symbolize reconciliation but acceptance into the club.

Another possible image candidate would show a couple of people (such as a married couple) who were about to tear each other to pieces until the minister raised his hands in a gesture of peace, so that the hostilities can begin to subside.

There is realism here in that people are often ready to tear one another to pieces. The trouble with this image, however, is that the minister seems to be using magic. One lift of the irenic arms and all is well. Further, the image suggests that the couple have not changed an iota of their feelings. They have simply been swayed by authority.

145

The image of the gavel seems superior to either that of the handshake or the irenic arms. In this image the minister is banging a gavel on the table, and a couple of people who have been waving their arms and yelling begin to subside.

The principal difference between this and the irenic-arms image is that functional ability within the context of law is shown as the reconciling medium, rather than charisma. The minister banging the gavel is moderating the meeting within an established context of law and procedure. This law gives everybody a chance to speak freely if he is decent, heeds the time schedule, and sticks to the point. No matter if a person is a minority, he may still speak. Neither he nor his opponent is required to agree. The reconciliation brought about by the gavel is not necessarily agreement. It may be only the first step of recalling heated participants to the law and the procedure. The one thing that is, in a way, forced is that recalling. Beyond this, other things will have to happen if the reconciling is to go further. But unless this is done, there is no possibility of such movement except by reversion to the charisma of the previous image. In the present image the freedom of the participants is not infringed. They simply have to do things decently and in order.

In its present form the handshake image would confuse, "I have nothing against you" (which may include indifference) with, "Despite what I have against you, I come now unarmed and ready to talk and listen."

The image of the minister with the charismatic arms would suggest either repression or keeping up appearances, not reconciliation, even if its apparent magic could be swallowed.

The gavel image is effective partly because it appears at an earlier point in the process of reconciling, partly because the sole authority is the reminder of consensus about procedure, and partly because the minister does not hesitate to use this kind of authority as relevant to the situation.

It may be argued that this image has nothing uniquely Christian about it, that it might just as well represent any democratic process. So far that is true. And if it is conceded that the church and minister have no short-cuts in these matters, then it might be well to place a Bible right beside the spot on the table where the minister bangs the gavel. Even a cross would not be out of place.

The Reconciling Process

Reconciling is a process rather than a conclusion at the human level. At the level of God's reconciling the world to himself through Jesus Christ, reconciling is both a conclusion and a once-for-all event as well as a process. Once the divinely appointed event has taken place, it is the context in which our human efforts at reconciling move. It is also a good part of our empowerment to continue. But it is in no way a substitute for the concrete processes through which we must move.

Some of our best knowledge of stages in the reconciling process has come through the modern study of small, face-to-face groups. Provided the group has a leader of competence who is neither authoritarian nor anarchic, the following, in a rough and general way, are the stages through which such a group moves.

1. At the start the group is polite and superficial, and is mildly for whatever party line it is meeting under. Nobody quite says what he really thinks. The leader accepts this level of discourse, is not fooled by it, is understanding of whatever is said, and may define the longer-term task to which the group addresses its efforts.

2. While presumably beginning to work on the task, various members in various ways try to get the leader on their side. He refuses to be so drawn, while at the same time he tries to understand the communication of each. He sees that they are so far not capable of communication with one another except through him.

3. Indirect expressions of hostility begin to emerge. Perhaps at first they are about the task, or a view some member has expressed. So far they are not usually directly against individual members. The leader may acknowledge directly some of these indirect attacks; but he is more likely to try to keep the climate going so that the person with the idea being attacked can begin to reply, not without emotion but with a sense that he is not "out" because of the concealed attack.

4. Speech becomes increasingly honest, including the anger,

147

hostility, and resentment. The expressions are more directly toward persons and positions. Eventually even the leader may be so addressed. Even while so speaking, various members may wonder when the group will blow up. So long as the discussions are decent, confined to the verbal level, and honest, the leader is pleased by the increasing expression of negative feeling.

5. To the surprise of everyone, respect by various members for various others increases. "I think your position is lousy, but I'm darned if I don't respect you for holding it as you do," would be a not unexpected comment at this stage. Once this procedure begins, it often has a charisma about it; and all members begin to look at all others in a new way.

6. One or another member begins to comment favorably upon this as a group and not simply as a task force or a collection of individuals. The mutual support of an emotional kind among members increases, even while they are going at one another hammer and tongs on content issues.

7. The content issues are worked on, by now with profit. The best knowledge and brains available are brought in and are respected. For the first time, genuine competence has its chance. Politics, however, has not become wholly defunct; but politics is a form of competence also.

8. With the task well along, nobody needs the group for the same reasons he did when he entered it. It may therefore be either dissolved or transformed.

One question will occur at once, upon reading these points, to the alert reader. What was needed as precondition to get the group there in the first place? That question is very basic, because it is evident that many of the situations that most need reconciling do not meet those starting conditions. Even if people are brought into the same room, there may be none of the disposition that could begin with point 1 and lead onward in the process.

Once the situation has reached the stage of the first point, then the lessons from group dynamics are of great significance. But we shall have to look elsewhere as to what you do if people won't begin at point 1.

Some additional light on the reconciling process has come from studies of counseling with married couples. One of my favorite role-playing situations in conferences of ministers and priests has found me assuming the role of minister or priest, while two of the participants are given the roles of a husband and wife with some written background about their character and how they fight. When the role-playing husband and wife approach the role-playing me, they begin to squabble. She, after all, had dragooned her husband into coming in the first place. She does most of the initial talking, all about what is wrong with her husband. He makes some nasty remarks and begins to retreat.

At that point the conferences expect me to say "You feel" and "I see" with such fervent effect that, very shortly, the husband and wife will be talking sense. They are generally shocked when they find me saying, "Now wait a minute. What you both seem to be doing is simply redoing before me about what you do in private. Each of you, in his own way, is obviously trying to win me to your side. That won't do. What I agreed to do was to try to help you with your marital situation. But in order to do so, we must get some kind of agreement on what we are trying to do, and not have this guerrilla warfare all over the place. Now, let me begin with you, Mrs. Blank. . . ." This procedure shocked a group of Roman Catholic priests even more than it had several sets of Protestant ministers. All of them had come to assume, since we correctly stress understanding in pastoral care and counseling, that given enough understanding, reconciling in the sense of "bring into harmony" would automatically evolve. This is, of course, not true.

My little object lesson through role-playing was drawn from actual experiences. The point is to know where you are in the process. Mrs. B. dragged Mr. B. to see the minister. Very well, he was dragged; but he did come—and that is part of the actual situation. Mrs. B. intended to have him trounced by the minister. Very well, but some part of her did want to re-create the marriage although another part simply wanted to save her pride. Should a minister *de facto* accept an implicit "contract" with such a couple in which he said only "I see," he would be making it impossible to help these people at this stage of their reconciling effort.

If, on the other hand, he is mindful of the gavel (which should be used only when needed), then he would be aware that right now the problem is not getting them to love each other more, but how to establish a procedure and a context in which their differences can be articulated and analyzed. Proceeding anarchically with no rules at all is not a stage of reconciling but acquiescence in a vague hope that something will turn up.

In many situations married couples will come to see the minister but wholly fail to see him as anything but a judge between them unless he makes it crystal clear at the start that this is not his role. Even then, some of them will leave. If they do, however, he need feel no more guilty about it than he would if he had to deny some other outrageous expectation. Once the minimal conditions are met, and some kind of context is accepted, then reconciling as a process at least has a chance if not a certainty. If the minimal conditions are not met, then one is only going through motions.

Among more sophisticated Christians there is a notion that, if you are having marital problems and decide to consult the minister or some other professional helper, you must at any cost show right off that you realize you may be partly at fault. "I know, doctor, that I haven't been as good to my wife as I should," is one illustration of this. To be sure, it may be genuine. But it is also an implicit, "Look, I am admitting that I have some faults. My wife won't admit to any, or at least to the right ones. Therefore, I am morally superior to her; and you, sir, as the arbiter, should acknowledge my superiority." Confession, we might say, is not enough even when it is genuine. So where do you go from here? This gentleman is not entirely wrong. But so long as his confession is a kind of bid for favor, it will impede the reconciling process unless it is as recognized as such.

I believe that the processes of reconciling that have been suggested through the group dynamics and the marriage counseling studies are generally valid beyond themselves—so long as the basic initial conditions can be met. But in terms of many of the most aggravated conflict situations within our culture, it is precisely these initial conditions that are not being met. Without being expert on any of this aspect of the problem, I shall try to make comment before I am finished. But the purpose of these efforts, which are so necessary, is to create the context in which

150

reconciling can begin as a process. When such efforts are misunderstood as the reconciling process itself, then harm is done. The reconciling process begins only when the group or groups are ready to talk together—no matter, at the start, about the ambiguity of their motivation, the concealment of their real concerns, or anything else. But getting up to that point is something other than what has been discussed so far.

There is a final point about the process of reconciling. The minister can expect and hope for so much that he may denigrate his own effective efforts that have moved a certain distance. Some years ago I was consulted by a couple of middle years. I found their own minister both able and cooperative, and he carried on from my own contact. The husband had had a period of hospitalization for a certain kind of psychic illness. Lately he had been doing well with his job and otherwise. But his wife was concerned that "he get the best possible help." Even though he was seeing a psychiatrist as needed, she said to me, "But if we could have a Christian psychiatrist, wouldn't it be better?"

Not only did I not think so, since this psychiatrist was doing an excellent job technically and also encouraging the couple's church participation. What bothered me was that the wife wanted her husband's problems solved permanently, that is, perfectionistically. But in all ways—financial, schedule-wise, psychologically, and so on—neither one would have been prepared for the major repair job that extended psychotherapy would have entailed. And if it had succeeded with him, he could probably not have returned to this rather dominating wife. So, in a way that was authoritative but not, I think, authoritarian, I gave them reassurance about the psychiatrist, got them back in touch with their own minister, and tried to get her off the perfectionistic slant about "curing" her husband. I believe this was realism.

I refuse to quote an incredible book I read years ago, according to which, if you were sufficiently convinced about reconciliation, you could handle mad dogs, boa constrictors, and grizzly bears. This kind of thinking confuses process with achievement; and in a less extreme form it is widespread in the church. Faith moving mountains is often cited as the text for such convictions. Faith has more important things to do, I believe, than being an inferior

151

bulldozer. And, granted that a calm personality can help you even with boa constrictors, I would suggest some special training to the aspirant.

As the psychoanalysts have put it, you are "overdetermined" when you become so preoccupied with the goals that you are reluctant about the steps in the process. A move from any stage to the next is equally to be desired—no matter where we start from.

This means that appraisal and evaluation of where we are now, where we begin from, is just as important to our aiding the reconciling process as is some apparent "coup." Go back, for instance, to the eight stages delineated about a small group movement of reconciliation. It was as important for the leader to appraise every stage correctly as it was for him to do all the other things that helped the group to move ahead. So it is, I think, with the minister in every process of reconciling.

Creating the Conditions for Reconciling to Start

Right in his own church, no matter where it is or what kind of members it has, every minister has a big job on his hands of getting reconciling going. Our discussion has dealt with this only through the counseling of couples and the potentiality of small groups. We have ignored teen-agers and their relation to parents, older people in their ambiguous relationship to those who run our society, and many other subjects for which church and ministry bear responsibility within the confines of the local parish.

But church and minister have responsibility for more than these. What, for instance, about reconciling in interracial relations? Specifically, what is the minister's responsibility for measures that may lead to the point where the processes of reconciling can go into operation? When I saw that excellent and realistic film, *A Time for Burning*, about a Lutheran church in Nebraska which tried to face up to its interracial obligations under the leadership of an able and courageous young minister, I welcomed the realistic descriptions and portrayals of conflict all through. But I was flabbergasted when the minister resigned. Whether he knew it or not, he had been helping to create the conditions in which the reconciling process can take place. But, exhausted, perhaps understandably, he had thrown in the towel, apparently unwilling to continue in the painful process without a timetable of clear success. I certainly admire greatly what he did—except for his failure of nerve at the end. And the end was by his own definition.

In interracial relations the recent riots have shown us two main things. The clearest and most obvious, and the one that the minister alone cannot do much about, is that there can be no true reconciling of the races until the opportunities for jobs, education, housing, and a general share in American prosperity are in actual fact available to members of all races. What the nation, the cities, and the states will do is still an open question. Here, ministers are citizens. As such, we may affect the issue. But we have nothing unique to bring.

The other point—as shown by the sociological report on the Watts riots of several years ago—is that severe discontent transcends sheer economics, jobs, and immediate opportunities to get ahead. It relates, rather, to a man's comparative status and acceptance among his fellow human beings. Some Negroes in Watts had jobs, houses, and reasonable incomes. But they still felt unaccepted—no doubt correctly. Alone, they would not have started riots. But let riots be begun by others lower in the economic scale, and they may join in, as some of them did.

I certainly have no formula for the church or the minister setting out to "accept" groups like Negroes. Indeed, if this is not tied up to doing something about the protests over various kinds of exclusions, it is a vain thought anyhow. Still, no matter how quietly it is done, anything at all that moves toward acceptance in actual fact is a move toward the point where the process of reconciling can begin. And reconciling is certainly not just adaptation to the status quo.

As to the reconciling of nations, I have no expertness at all, only concern. Happily, our church councils seem to be maintaining their courage on these matters and also getting, latterly, more competent technical advice.

I am deeply concerned about the relations among the religions of the world. At Princeton Seminary in 1966 we had a World

153

Religions Conference, which was small enough to be face to face and which included scholars and believers from all the great religions of the world. In days past, we could regard these persons and beliefs as "esoterica," suitable objects of scholarship by odd professors but otherwise of not much concern to our own religious life.

This patronizing attitude can no longer be sustained. Buddhism in its various branches, Islam, Hinduism, Taoism, and others of the long-estabished religious faiths—plus new religions all over the world and the so-called primitive or local religions of Africa and elsewhere—are all now of world concern. Can we create the conditions under which reconciling ourselves with them is possible? The question is not so much the reconciling process itself, but whether we have sufficient concern to create the context in which they might be interested to enter upon reconciliation processes with us. Or ourselves with them—which may be the basic issue.

On all such questions the minister may say, as I indeed say to myself: "Look, you aren't an expert in this. So why not let the church experts take care of it?" The trouble is that the "experts" are still awaiting leads from their constituency. If nobody suggests that they take Islam seriously and try to enter into dialogue with some of its leaders, they become hesitant. Why should it not be the job of the minister to tell the experts of his church: "Talk seriously with Islam"? The result could mean more than most ministers may realize.

When Reconciling Cannot Be Started

What does a minister do when one member of a married couple comes to him about marital conflict but reports that the spouse refuses to come along? This is a frequent question, and a good many ministers are inclined to say that we cannot do anything until the spouse can be persuaded to come. I regard such a conclusion as both unwarranted and dangerous.

The fact is that the spouse who does come herself has a problem. Suppose, for instance, that her husband is an alcoholic. His alcoholism is threatening many things, including the marriage.

And nobody can know what his eventual fate will be. The basic problem of his wife is that she must plan her life so that it is not in all respects contingent upon what happens to him. This could not be done with the husband present. It may be done with her alone. Yet she is so obtrusively preoccupied with trying to get a solution to her husband's problem that she will not, unless helped, see what her own problem is.

When she is so aided, however, we ordinarily find that the "disengagement" she begins to achieve from her husband's problem and the marital problem may be of some indirect help to him. He cannot, however unconsciously, quite "use" her as he had done before. Thus, her courage in getting help for herself tends to increase the chance of creating the conditions under which the reconciling process becomes possible. But if those conditions do not emerge, there are aspects of her life and her self-respect that can stand up—even if her husband goes on downhill. She will not be using the desire for reconciliation as a club over herself, and will not feel guilty when the conditions fail to appear.

In many kinds of situations there has to be an apparent move backward from the reconciling process in order to have a chance of creating the conditions in which it may begin. The story above illustrates this point. Quite possibly the wife said early to the minister, "But I thought you ministers were interested in saving marriages." The minister must be prepared in advance to deal with such charges.

Another illustration is the not infrequent discovery by a minister that one member of his church's official board is absolutely recalcitrant on every issue. Certainly a minister will explore first all reasonable means of understanding such a person and the positions he takes. But the kind of person I am thinking of becomes more obdurate under such kindly but loose treatment, and I have seen many ministers who have spent hours of guilty self-reflection over their "failure to reconcile" such persons. Actually, such people are likely to be, in the technical definition, "authoritarian personalities" who may be "contained" but who are incapable of being reconciled. Firmness along with kindness may prevent them from injuring the group. But this is possible only when the minister quits feeling guilty because he has not got them reconciled.

The stepping back is not at the point of conviction and principle, but at that of direct effort to bring about the starting base from which reconciling processes might proceed. The opposite of this kind of stepping back was the historical figure of Prime Minister Neville Chamberlain at the Munich conference with Adolf Hitler, declaring, after he had followed an appeasement line, that this meant peace in our time.

Because we ministers rightly believe that involvement in the reconciling process is a central task, we are more reluctant than most people to step back when, at least for the time being, the initial conditions for that process are not present. We want a rebellious teen-ager to understand his parents, and his parents to understand him. We want to reconcile them. But in our kind of society it may be that the adolescent can win the necessary emotional freedom from his parents only if, for the time being, he is permitted some distance from them. This may be where the parents crucially learn that the pain of giving their children up emotionally is more important than future happy visits from grandchildren.

Finally, I believe that we ministers should recognize that there are some good devices, occasionally used in the church as well as in society, which help to reduce conflict even when reconciling cannot get off the ground. Between management and workers there are collective bargainings and, if necessary, arbitrations. In international relations there is a variety of methods. Most church rules of order (except perhaps the Quakers) make provision for getting ahead even when reconciling has proved impossible. With these last we are often apologetic, as if our hands were dirty when full reconciliation could not be effected. This seems to me an error. Granted the depth and actuality of the differences, the solutions may well be the will of the Lord. To pine uselessly about full reconciliation deflects proper attention from the procedures that are possible.

The problem that has been under discussion is, of course, a part of the larger question of the relationship between love and justice. In those terms my argument has been (along with that of Reinhold Niebuhr) that overpreoccupation with love may make us inattentive to our duty to establish justice. In very many situations justice is not second-best to love but, as Joseph Fletcher rightly says, as much love as the situation can contain.

10
The Ministry as Theologizing

With due respect to Roman Catholicism, to which the idea is not now alien, it is nevertheless a unique emphasis in Protestantism that every minister is to be a theologian. However important the things he does—preaching, shepherding, administering, teaching, evangelizing, and the like—he is also to think and inquire. He may and should pay attention to the thought and inquiry of others who may be more gifted than he. But no matter how great their expertness, he is not to follow it slavishly as if his is not to reason why. Thus his ministry includes theologizing as an active process. No more than any other function of ministry is theologizing to be set apart by itself, or interpreted out of context. But in that context it is indispensable, not merely preparation but ministry itself. This conception of church leadership is unique to Christianity; and the emphasis on it is unique to Protestantism.

If our focal concern in this book were the church rather than the ministry, we should be obliged to point out that in some basic sense every Christian is expected in Protestantism to be a theologian. He is himself, for instance, to read the Bible and, with expert help, to try on his own to understand it. He is not to sit passively and leave its interpretation to others. Thus there is a theological obligation on the part of every Christian, especially to back up universal priesthood and Christian vocation. But this degree of obligation does not absolve the ordained minister of special theological obligations. It is indeed part of his obligation as minister to evoke the theologizing of other Christians, but he can hardly use their participation in it as an excuse for getting out of it himself. Our concern here is with the ordained minister. An elucidation of his obligation to theologize is certainly not to be read as an excuse for laymen not to participate. But laymen are not our point of reference here.

Reluctant Theologians

The evidences of what this emphasis upon the minister as theologian has done are very widespread in the history of the past four centuries. The immense Protestant contribution to education at virtually all levels is incomprehensible without it. Our own American colleges were first founded to raise up men for the ministry, and it was explicitly defined as a "learned ministry," not training in a trade without ability to think and theologize. At least until our own century ministers were generally regarded as the most learned men in town. Printing, publication, and other means of public communication were also stimulated by this conviction.

And yet, if a Gallup poll were done of ministers of all denominations with the question, "Do you regard yourself as a theologian?" the results would probably emerge as follows:

31% said, "Well, I am a minister, but you could hardly call me a theologian."

22% said, "It is true I have studied theology, but I'm not really a theologian."

17% replied, "Brother, I sure ain't. I'm only a simple parson, not one of those high-powered book guys."

8% admitted, "Well, I guess I am, in a way, but I am more interested in serving people than in theology."

7% said, "Where did you get that idea? And don't do it again. I'd even rather be called 'Reverend' than 'theologian.' "

5% said, "No."

4% replied, "I am about twice a year, when I go back for the alumni lectures."

2% said, "Pardon me, I have to rush to a funeral."

1% snorted, "I wonder who thought up that question?"

2% alleged, "I can see that someone from Princeton Seminary has been propagandizing George Gallup."

0.9% said, "Yes."

What does this contradiction mean? Why do most ministers deny that they are theologians, even though the requirement that every minister be a theologian is the functionally unique emphasis of Protestantism among the religions of the world? Certainly a partial answer to this question comes from common sense: that the notion of "theology" has come to have academic and specialized meanings from which a general practitioner, with some justice, excludes himself. On this matter the specialists are not innocent. They have, in two ways, intimidated ministers into disassociating themselves as theologians. First, they have taught the various branches of theology so academically in seminaries that the students come to regard all theology as the work only of specialists, and apparently nonministering ones at that. Second, while acknowledging that the ministry is a good place to use theology, they have not admitted that it also involves theological construction, and hence have helped remove from the minister any sense that he is a creative participant in the larger theological enterprise. Thus the minister comes to feel like a salesman who gets his products from the factory by way of the warehouse, but who would answer "no" to the question about his creative participation in making the product.

A proper study of this matter would demonstrate very complex historical reasons behind this reluctance of ministers to admit either that they are theologians or that their theologizing is a part of their ministering. Without professing to be in any way exhaustive, and still keeping the cartoon images focally before us, we can get inside some of these historical reasons by examining implicit images that ministers in various circumstances have been rejecting when they were reluctant theologians.

We may begin, for example, with a certain tradition within the Church of England, in which the minister or priest performed his liturgical, homiletical, and pastoral duties, and perhaps even did spots of reading about them, but in which his serious continuing intellectual work along some particular line might have little or nothing to do with theology. One thinks, for example, of

Bishop Berkeley's mathematics and philosophy. At least through a good part of the nineteenth century, a great deal of the specialized scholarship in nearly all fields was done by clergymen in England, not as the center of their jobs but as the intellectual accompaniment to their work of ministering.

My guess is that the image these men and this tradition were rejecting was that of the "hired man." Generally speaking, the income level and social status of Anglican clergy was not high. One was often at the mercy of the local lord or squire or, even more ghastly, of his wife. To be sure, the primary duties of ministry were seldom subject to arbitrary manipulation; but feelings about churchmanship could often be nudged up or down a few degrees on the high-low scale. How, under such pressures, could clergymen effectively retain their sense that they were not just hired men but also learned ministers? For this purpose, expertness in some branch of theology might be quite inferior to a serious pursuit of mathematics, or classical literature, or archaeology, or botany. If such a person were asked whether he were a theologian, he could reply, "I am a priest, and also a kind of mathematician." This may not always have been a bad thing, although it did tend to leave many of the functions of ministry uncriticized from various important theological perspectives. For it often took the heat off the need to find focus, interest, and status entirely through the functions and relationships of ministry, and thus no doubt contributed to mental health.

If we turn to one important development in the history of the ministry in our own country, we may think, for instance, of one of its important representatives in the person of circuit-riding Peter Cartwright. No doubt he would have replied negatively if asked about his being a theologian. Or else he would have said, "I am a theologian only to the extent that I study the Bible daily, even while on horseback." What Cartwright would have been reacting against, in image terms, was the picture of a fixed, settled, and shielded person not moving about the migrating world to bring the gospel of Jesus Christ to people who need it. He might also have been suspicious of all the other books in the study of the settled minister as endangering the all-sufficiency of the Bible.

It hardly needs elaboration that both these considerations have been prominent in the development of ministry in America.

In German-speaking countries and in Scandanavia there was still another kind of tradition. Whether or not the university-educated minister did in fact continue his scholarly pursuits alongside the work of his parish, he was encouraged to do so and was often evaluated positively to the degree that he did so. The subject of his continuing studies was usually either a branch of theology or something that theology had given rise to, such as Oriental languages or history. Since most of his studies in university days were in the traditional fields of theology, his later pursuit of a special theological subject was ordinarily within the traditional fields. Even today, visiting Americans are surprised at how many German or Swiss ministers are fully up to date about Barth's or Bultmann's latest, even to the extent of being able to write learned reviews with all the technical paraphernalia.

What differentiates this situation from the older Anglican one is that the specialties here pursued are alleged to be theological in character. But the definitions of what is theological have seldom included emerging fields and concerns and have usually been conceived traditionally. What seems to be argued for implicitly in this tradition is the positive assertion, "I am a scholar; a scholar is one who pursues a specialized field; and since I am a theological scholar, what I am pursuing is a special field of theology." In reply to the question, "Are you, then, a theologian?" such a person would reply "yes" only if his special field were doctrinal theology. Otherwise he would say, "I am a New Testament scholar," or "My field is medieval church history." In other words, the positive image is to show that, even though one is not literally within the groves of Academe, his robe and his pen are still as dominant in his vocational self-image as if he were a professor. Another proof of this is the status accorded even theological professors in German and Scandanavian cultures.

I hope I do our Continental brethren no injustice in suggesting that this tradition has also, implicitly, rejected a particular image. That image seems to me to be the servant image, when servant-hood is understood as functional in nature. If service is as service does, then that seems to be the image rejected by this part of the

Continental tradition. To be sure, the minister must perform certain functions; but what is important about even the functions is not their function but something else: their authority, their source, or the knowledge from which they proceed. This fact helps to explain why the "custodian" image of the ministry, to use the phrase of a Dutch scholar, Heije Faber, has been so prominent on the Continent and appears so strange in America.

In America the reluctance of the minister to be a theologian is also a product of the anti-intellectual aspects of American culture. To this stream of American life intellectualism means pretentiousness or potential arrogance. If you are an intellectual in America, you have two ways in which you may proceed without being rejected. The first is to be obviously successful. In that event, you are out of the competition. You become a father or a lord instead of participating in sibling rivalry. If successful, your actions that otherwise would have been regarded as condescending now become thoughtful. The other path is to prove you are one of the boys; or, in sibling-relation terms, that you know you are no smarter than anyone else. It is a curious thing how the sibling rivalry motif is so deeply involved with our anti-intellectualism.

We have seen, then, a sampling of the images that various traditions of the ministry have rejected when reluctant, on one count or another, to accept the responsibility of being theologians. The full story would go much more deeply than our samples. But for present purposes, we can see how such images as the hired man, the functional servant, the unadventurous bookman, or the pretentious highbrow have been involved in the rejection of responsibility as theologian. Theologian, then, has become ambiguous, and theologizing incomprehensible. We shall turn to ask if there is another image or images, actually or potentially more positive, of the minister as theologian that may help us deal with the contradiction that now exists between the clear Protestant call for the minister to be a theologian and his reluctance to accept the charge.

The Passive Theologian Image

The older Protestant image of the minister as theologian was, or appeared to be, passive. The minister sat reading his Bible.

163

To be sure, "reading" is an active and transitive verb. But the thrust of the image was that the Bible, or the Word of God through the Bible, struck the minister as he read. He was a theological recipient. But is a theological recipient a theologian? Indeed, is a passive recipient a faithful or competent recipient? If he appears to receive, but has no pen in hand to make notes against the fallibility of his own memory or the evanescence of profound insight, is he really taking seriously what he professes to receive?

In actual fact, the passive image of reading the Bible seldom occurs alone in Protestantism. It is nearly always followed at once by the image of preaching we have already noted, by a teaching image, or by some other image of function and service such as that of shepherding. The Word through the Bible may indeed strike the minister recipient, which is as it should be. But he does not just go on sitting. He responds in action, in service, in communication, and in testimony. Nevertheless, despite this inescapable linkage of theological receptivity and response through function, this image is dubious. It could have characterized no leader of Protestant thought or work. Luther did not just read the Bible. He also translated it. Metaphorically speaking, one cannot imagine Calvin without pen in hand as he read. Such men were clearly aware that theologizing was an active process, whether they were making notes, writing sermons, compiling commentaries, or writing letters. Even Luther's table talk is theologizing. Surrender was an attitude toward God, not an invitation to passivity. One could not even grasp the meaning of surrender without reworking it. Hence the old theologian image was always inadequate to the best theologians.

Nor does the old image lose its passivity when some aspects of its context are made explicit. We can, for example, add the following items to it, since they were always implicit. We can show the minister in a book-lined study, reading and being guided by the Bible, but consulting other works which may be important even in understanding the Word through the Bible. This addition does, in principle, guard against a bibliocentrism that may distort our understanding of the biblical message itself. It is good, but it does not transcend passivity.

We may also add to our Bible-reading image a typewriter. This suggests that the modern minister, technically speaking, is not confined to the technologies of the past. He may write his sermons so that cryptography is unnecessary in reading them. And yet, although this too is good, passivity remains. He seems only to be more efficient and clearer in passing on what he has received.

The minister and his desk may be shown before a window. And through the window we may see perhaps the smoke of industry, the log jam of traffic, the uproar of a football game, or the grimy ruin of inner-city slums. By this addition we may show that the Word is for the world, to rejoice when it rejoices, to bind up its wounds when in pain, to rescue it from barbarity and attrition and impoverishment. This too is good, and it does imply that something is finally needed beyond passivity. But as to the intellectual aspects of the task, there is still nothing beyond passivity. Action? Yes. But an active and creative dimension of thought and reflection after being struck by the Word? The image does not say so.

Even if we move to the various specialist images of the theologian, we remain in the realm of passivity. The biblical scholar crouched over scrolls or archaeological remnants, the doctrinal theologian holding an earthen vessel that he at least believes to contain a treasure, the moral theologian stoutly defending something or other against something else, or the historical theologian looking like the Connecticut Yankee in somebody's ecclesiastical backyard—all are doing something and in that sense are active. But there is nothing in such images that suggests the *theologizing* as active. The response to it is indeed active. But what comes between hearing and doing? Apparently not much of consequence.

To a frightening extent, the modern arrogation of the title "theologian" to seminary professors with doctor's degrees, Latin styles, German specialisms, concealed inferiority complexes, and a conviction that they have been "elevated" from the ministry of the local church is now exacerbating the long-standing condition. We Americans are charged with being activists. But what American has the courage to try writing a systematic theology in any field: doctrine, Bible, ethics, history, or otherwise? Only Paul Tillich and Nels Ferré have even tried it, and Tillich's roots were

German while Ferré's intent to be systematic is still in doubt. It is surely not that we lack theological minds of high scholarship, efficient capacity for work, or ability to find publishers. It is rather that such active intent to acknowledge theologizing as perpetual reconstruction appears pretentious, overambitious, getting too big for one's hood, and other successfully self-intimidating motivations. The result is that the scholarship of American activists is astonishingly passive. On smaller and more partial matters, it is becoming astonishingly good. And there is more of it than ever. But who really sticks his neck out, except Tillich and Ferré? Most academic theologians obtrude a little finger. A few risk one hand. But all seem terrified of sibling rivalry.

This apparent humility that is actually passivity is tempted to even greater extremes as our academic institutions become larger, cultivate more specialized faculties, and thus make possible more accurate teaching and scholarship and more penetrating specialized inquiry. The retreat into professed ignorance but for one's specialty may appear, on the surface, like that of the Germans. But whatever one may say against the Germans in theology, they have not lacked intellectual guts, vigor, and a disposition to very active articulation and controversy. Our situation is now tempted with the bad side of German theological scholarship, without assimilating the other side that has been its glory.

Although I have enjoyed these last few moments of spanking the professors, which is *my* way of dealing with sibling rivalry, my concern is with the way in which what is happening to theology in academic circles is infecting ministers generally. So long as those who call themselves theologians are essentially passive, what they communicate about the nature of theologizing is also essentially passive. Not that most ministers understand what is happening to them. "He understands Barth and Bultmann, and I don't," implies that understanding those gentlemen is itself a sufficiently active process to be worthy of the term "theology." But the fact is that anyone who understands either or both of those gentlemen, and who is not champing at the bit to make the needed corrections in their views, is either brainless or passive. The view of theology actually insinuated is rather more like that of a competent language translator than of an active and creative

166

reworker of man's assimilation of the faith. A translator can be most impressive; his skill may be very great. But all his skill and competence cannot conceal the fact that he has few ideas of his own.

I am often amused by the irony of, above all others, Karl Barth declaring, in twelve long and complex and very active volumes, that man can simply trust in, receive, and be struck by the Word of God—especially when, with a manner so confident that he can afford to be utterly calm, he explains the desirability of such passive attitudes to American ministers who have driven hundreds of miles, raised a few extra dollars for gasoline, and bound up a few wounds on the way while feeling guilty throughout the journey that they have not diligently yielded themselves to the discipline of the twelve volumes. I believe Peter Cartwright would have done better than that by Barth. With those long rides of his, he might even have got through the twelve volumes, always regarding them, of course, as recreational reading between his bouts with the Bible. At any rate, I cannot imagine him being passive at a Barth lecture. Either he would be, next day, preaching with the help of a Barth who had convinced him or analyzing in his diary where Barth was fudging. But in neither event would he be passive.

I frankly doubt that the professors will acknowledge and correct this growing passivity on their own. But suppose that many ministers, and not just the professor theologians, become convinced not only that they too are and must be theologians but also that theologizing is part of their ministry? Then, I think, even we professors may listen.

The Functional Theologian Image

Many historians of science have noted that the progression of subjects to which science has turned its attention has been rather steadily from the remote toward the proximate. Scientific astronomy preceded scientific psychology. The reasons for this sequence are severely complex. They are not mere reluctance over self-exposure, although such a motive is indeed present. They certainly include a distrust that the close, the proximate, and the commonplace are worthy of study in the same sense as the majestic stars, the mystifying atom, or the intriguing developments of biological or linguistic evolution.

So far as I know every science in its infant days has put its principal attention upon what seemed most strikingly different from the commonplace. Cultural anthropology went to Samoa before it invaded Japan or New York. The psychology of religion studied adolescent conversions before it asked why the psychologist left fundamentalism and became a Quaker, an Episcopalian, or a Unitarian. Professional sociology is still much more revealing about the interior workings of all social classes except the professional. Only the natural sciences have moved far enough to realize that the macroscopic and the microscopic are actually close together, that the road to objectivity demands the steady clarification of subjectivities, and that what may have seemed remote may actually be nearer than breathing and closer than endocrine glands.

Although it ought to know better, theology has generally succumbed to the same temptation. It has usually felt more at home with the theological equivalent of astronomy than with the opposite number of psychology, geniuses like Augustine always excepted. To the respectable, what happened then has always seemed more worthy of study than what is happening now. The illusion that the now is either so insignificant and commonplace as to be unworthy of study, or that it is so well known anyhow—without analysis, critical reflection, or even systematic observation—as to be beneath serious notice, has become all too characteristic of a theological tradition that knows perfectly well that we cannot understand either God's grace or man's sinfulness without in some fundamental sense understanding the other first.

The creative theologians of our day—including, each in its own way, Barth, Brunner, Bonhoeffer, Bultmann, Niebuhr, Tillich, and others—have all moved in their *content* in the direction of acknowledging the importance of analyzing the commonplace, the near, or even the functional. I confess freely that some of them do it backhandedly. But they all do it to some degree. But when we examine their *methods*, we find quite a different story. Barth includes in his content things that are not permitted by his method. Tillich promises in his method things that never appear in his content. The great uniqueness of Niebuhr, his social science perspective on theological questions, is constantly deprecated by him; or else, when in one of his self-depreciative moods, he claims he is not a theologian. That is nonsense, but it is nonsense based on the error that insight into function is an inferior form of theory.

Let me return to the minister at work, in the hope that these comments on the history of science and the ideologies of theology can be connected up. What does this minister do, for instance, when he is driving back to the church after making a hospital call, or driving home after a frustrating committee meeting at the church, or flying home after a freedom march or an assault on poverty? Unless he is perfectly adapted to the ministry, in which event he should be selling something somewhere, he is certainly being reflective about what he has just gone through. Whatever the specific nature of the situation he has just left, he did not respond to it in detached fashion. He was, and is, involved. It meant something to him. He felt, and still feels, it. He may, of course, have only the rudimentary and uncritical reflections from his feelings, concluding that he did well because he feels good or that he failed because he is still concerned. But let us assume that he has some transcendence over such subjectivities. In that event, he is truly appraising what happened and why, not sparing the egoistic horses but primarily with an eye to the next occasion. He may, as many ministers actually are, be conducting the most rigorous and penetrating kind of professional self-appraisal that will indeed improve what he tries to do next time. Such moments may be, for him, the hurting but helping true learning experiences of his ministry. They may be, in actual fact, the most penetrating theologizing he ever does. And yet, despite their benefit to him and to his people and to the church and to the Kingdom of God, it may seem to him utterly bizarre and eccentric to say that he is here engaged in a kind of creative theologizing that even a Barth should envy.

Let me be clear that I am not baptizing subjective feelings as theologizing. If the minister has not read and studied the Bible, gone to theological seminary and learned about other branches of theology, acquired an insight and a skill or two along the way, and seen what he was trying to do in a context appropriate to the ministry of the Christian church, none of what I am asserting would follow. The context and the conditions are indispensable. But if they are present, and if the critical reflection is as suggested, then we have in fact an active and creative theologizing that should have no inferiority complex before the big B's, the professors, or even God himself. For Job, the psalmist, Paul, and the prophets, whatever their particular concerns, were never passive theologians even before God himself. And they all came round to theologizing about the commonplace and the familiar.

I would readily agree that theologizing is not merely reflective meditation about immediate functions or events, apart from the context in which these are seen, the motives with which they are approached, and the perspective that one brings. But, granted those conditions, then reflection upon them—in that context, with those motives, and with that perspective—is fully as much an act of theologizing as any apprehension that strikes us out of the Bible, or Bultmann, or Barth, or any other alphabetical characters past or present. This kind of reflection is theologizing; it is also ministry, for it cannot be done except in the context of preparing for future occasions of function and service. It ought to be ruthless in its subjectivity. "Why *did* I drag in that old saw at that point?" But this is toward an objective end. "Next time at least I won't do that, in the light of. . . ." Right or wrong, and in whatever degree, what can be more theologically responsible than that? Or, if he got it right, more creative?

To my entire line of argument, you may of course reply, "Very good. If the minister is preaching properly, shepherding people effectively, building up the body of Christ along with other Christians, that is great. But why all this business about making theology out of it? Why not let us get on with the task? Why give it such a fancy and highbrow name? That's all right for those fellows at Princeton, Basel, Göttingen, and Edinburgh. But all we want is to help our people, to be instruments of mediating the Word and the finger of God to these human, likable, troubled, and sinful people. Why fuss us up with theology?"

Why indeed? The answer is that theology is a very human, and very important, enterprise; that grasping and assimilating what God has done and continues to do is not something that can be engaged in passively but is a challenge to everything any of us possesses; that the separation of theologizing from what the minister and the church try, fallibly but authentically, to hear of the Word of God in specific situations from some alleged and remote theology is bound to be blasphemous as well as mistaken; and that the one way to hear the Word of God, if it contains the Protestant principle, is to submit our functions to concrete self-criticism. But, if any of this is done, it is not just psychology or sociology or philosophy or linguistics or technology, however competent; it is also, in the quite precise sense, theology. And if it is sifted and criticized and verbalized, and submitted for criticism, it may become some form of systematic theology.

The minister is also a theologian, and theologizing in its proper context is an aspect of ministry. Go thou and do likewise. And then, as even Thomas J. Watson has counseled us, THINK. The result just might be theology.

11
The Ministry as Disciplining

I have used the term "disciplining" after much hesitation and reflection, and a final decision that nothing else will take its place. Like most moderns, I once thought all the connotations of "discipline" were about what parents and teachers did to you when you failed to conduct yourself as they thought you should. Discipline was very close to punishment.

Even when I learned, rather early, that "discipline" and "disciple" were supposed to be closely related, I could connect these ideas only through the notion of "self-discipline." And while that was supposed to be a good thing, its connotations were all about what you ought not to do.

I have become allergic to slick modern interpretations of discipline that bear down heavily on discipleship and ignore the long series of historical events that moved the focus of the term from a glad and voluntary commitment and placed it around censure of the individual by the group. In this discussion no such legerdemain is permitted.

In the process of my slow reconciliation to the term I have been especially aided by experts in child study, who have been redefining discipline as protection of the child from that from which he is not yet ready to protect himself. In this most elementary area of parent-child relationships, such a notion rescues discipline from connotations of punishment and has the further virtue of counseling foresight, according to which the best disciplining parent is the one who anticipates that from which the child alone cannot protect himself and does something about it before the child is injured. In this child-care sense, then, discipline

172

as redefined is a kind of shepherding function, with preventive aspects emphasized. To be sure, if the child does something that needs to be stopped, this is still discipline also. But the focus is now before rather than after the fact of error.

Still thinking of discipline in terms of child care, it becomes apparent, however, that the best prevention is education whenever it can be achieved; that is, that the child who can learn to anticipate consequences for himself is in a much better position to avoid harmful misconduct than the child who relies wholly on external admonitions. The aim of discipline is, then, always in the direction of capacity for self-discipline. But self-discipline in this sense is not merely negative, refraining from fun. It is alert self-protection from harm; or, still more positively, discovering and pursuing what will do more good.

Whether the term "discipline" can survive these conflicts and shifts I do not know. But for purposes of the present discussion, I shall assume that it has a chance.

When disciplining is seen in this way, then the topics for subsequent discussion become clear. They fall into two general categories: the minister's disciplining of himself, in both his personal and his professional dimensions, to the intent of making his ministry effective; and the minister's attempts, with other people, to evoke appropriate self-discipline. These will be considered in turn.

The Image of Disciplining

Now that we know what we are looking for, I believe there is a nascent image in Protestantism of the ministry as disciplining. It is a fuzzy cartoon. It shows a minister in an unmistakable attitude of praying, and that much is not obscure. The fuzziness is because other possible images impinge, like a double or a triple exposure on a film. Why prayer and not study and action? Why the minister by himself? Why is he not disciplining others, at least in the sense of aiding them to move in the direction of self-discipline? These other potential images are not against the minister's praying. But they are competing for the model of the ministry as disciplining.

173

I want to defend this simple image of the minister praying as central to disciplining. We must first, however, give instructions to our cartoonist. Let him choose as to whether the minister is kneeling, seated, or standing. So long as his head is bowed, he is in the attitude of prayer. But the surroundings are important. There should be some clear Christian symbol, such as a Bible or a cross or a prayer book, in the proper place. But since prayer is not purely for the self or for the church, but also for others and for the needs of the world, something in the cartoon should suggest this relevance. Perhaps again the device of the window could be useful. Even though the minister's head is bowed, the cartoon can show through the window some smoke or confusion or dirt. Although the minister does not, in the prayer stance, actually see these symbolic problems of the world, he can be shown as faced in that direction. This rescues his praying from mere ecclesiasticism, and also from self-preoccupation.

Presenting the minister by himself in this image is for the same reasons as in the image of the minister as theologian. As theologian, he was preparing himself through study. Eventually he would make available the results of his reflection to other people. But the critical point of the image was his processes of reflection— the production rather than the sales. The same requirement holds for the image of disciplining. Eventually he will be conveying something to others. But what is crucial are the processes by which he gets it himself.

The image is about prayer not because prayer is the sole way of discipline, but rather because it is the procedure not highlighted by the other images. Discipline comes also through study, and there we have the ministry as theologizing. It comes, further, through action, and there the ministry is reconciling. But the base and the energizer for even these is prayer, the minister humbly but honestly speaking and listening to God—in thanksgiving, confession, petition, and intercession.

When it comes to private praying, my record is about like that of most ministers—a rather feeble, lower-case average with occasional spurts into capital letters, especially when things get tough. I do have two gimmicks about my own praying, which may or may not be relevant to others. The first is laying before

God periodically, i.e., daily, a "feeling review" of the events, encounters, and thoughts of the period and trying to hear the appraisal that comes from this presentation. The second is a similar procedure about the events of ministry, those that have touched other people and not merely myself—and to the same end of articulating for myself and trying to hear the discriminating evaluation. Like anybody else who prays at all, in times of special need I throw all regularities to the winds and just let loose. But I try never to overlook, even in time of deep personal need, the concomitant professional obligations.

I confess that there was a period in my life when I wondered if praying was merely a historically sanctioned procedure for challenging me to bring the separate aspects of my psyche into some kind of integration. I began to quit worrying about such an interpretation when I realized that God himself regarded this as a good thing—if it could be managed. That realization made God more real to me, in both his immanent concern and his transcendent otherness. But in prayer all this is impossible without corollary concern for others and for the world. And that, for the ordained minister, means praying about his professional exercise of responsibility as well as about his Christian faith.

Self-Disciplining: The Personal Self

There is no need to repeat the common sense on these matters that has been said by many writers far better than I could say it. Despite all the helter-skelter of schedules in the modern minister's home, some kind of regularity about devotional practices makes sense. It does no good to one's ministry to take no time out from it for family and hobbies and just sheer recreation. If the minister finds that he has unresolved personal or family problems, let him seek help on these like anyone else. Let the study that is to be for long-term improvement not be wholly displaced by that which confronts the deadline of next Sunday's sermon. And so on. All these things are sound advice.

I believe, however, that we ministers face unusual problems these days in the personal aspects of self-discipline. It is not that we are unprepared to exercise it if we were sure what it should

175

be about. But not being very sure, we develop our patterns rather opportunistically. Because of that fact, it does not feel like "self-discipline"; and so we vaguely hope that some better situation may come along someday and repair everything, while all the while habit patterns are being ingrained—be they of self-flagellation or self-indulgence. And when we make a move in some area to create a new pattern, there is likely to be enough ambiguity about it to make us retreat.

Take personal friendship as an illustration. The chances are that the young minister had a couple of good friends while in seminary, not counting his wife. But when he becomes immersed in full-time ministry, and the job is never done, and he has not prayed enough nor done enough for his family, the chances are that he develops "hosts of friends" but has no real friend, even another minister, with whom he can share the gripes that one does share only with a real personal friend. Since friendship of this kind develops organically and not on command, he probably finds, as time goes on, that friendship begins with a person or two. But he may not let it develop. "You can't be real friends with one of your parishioners," he may have heard, and he may have swallowed this propaganda. Or the person may be an agnostic; and what would the congregation think if they found that out?

I am certainly not against the minister's duties to and pleasures with his wife and children. But if the minister comes to feel disloyal or unfaithful at having a real friend other than his wife, then it makes wife and family carry a burden that is very heavy for all but the most rare of spouses. And yet there is a strong pressure on the minister to feel such disloyalty. One of the unsung virtues of our many continuing education ventures these days is that ministers can get away from these patterns for a short time, and not infrequently begin to take a new look at friendship.

Close friendship is mutuality. It is an acknowledgment that I need something from you, and not merely that I am big enough to give something to you. The pressures upon the minister tend to make him feel, however, that he should be big enough to give out all the time except at home. This is simply false. Nobody is as strong as that. In one sense, to need a couple of close friends

176

is to admit weakness. Well, why not? This seems an appropriate part of personal self-disciplining.

There is a certain amount of personal self-disciplining in relation to one's family that does tend, these days, to come about naturally, even with the minister's schedule. There is the post-dinner period with the children, unless television gets out of hand. There is the summer vacation, the trip to the grandparents, the going out to dinner if a baby sitter can be found, and much else.

In most places these days a minister's wife and children are permitted to be themselves, so that some of the older kinds of pressures are either gone or greatly reduced. But the minister is under strong internal pressure to be the "good father." Thus, no matter what his schedule with his family, he is tempted either to smugness or guilt—both equally harmful. He may find himself, on home evenings, so exhausted by the time the children are in bed that he can do nothing but flop in front of the television set.

Again, the minister is under pressure to feel guilty if he develops anything like a serious hobby. A hobby is a continuing interest involving some commitment of time, energy, and skill—but not for profit. It is potentially "re-creative" as passive participations are not. And I think more ministers have hobbies today. I wish someone had encouraged me, when I began my ministry, to keep up my amateur interest in music. They didn't, and I later got on to carpentry—which is not as good for culture but a lot better for unloading hostility. The point I am making is that reasonable pursuit of a hobby is a part of personal self-discipline, rather than an enemy of it. I think the Lord loveth a cheerful amateur carpenter.

Finally, as to the how of personal prayer and devotional life, I have only one suggestion. Find out what is realistic and meaningful for you; and don't be stampeded into guilt or apathy by those persons who believe that the more prayer the better. Beyond passing out daily devotional booklets, we are not very competent in Protestantism in guiding individually the devotional life of our parishioners. Thus, we tend to think collectively rather than individually even about ourselves; and the two distortions tend to reinforce each other. Whatever you do, figure it out for yourself.

Self-Discipline: The Professional Self

Although the terms "profession" and "professional" are used in many ways—to show you get paid or that it is your job, like a golf "pro," for instance—the real meaning of professional is "responsibility." It is not privilege, not impersonality, and not money, but basically the exercise of responsibility—in certain ways. So understood, the minister is a professional man.

In summary form, here are the features necessary to a profession and a professional man.

1. He works on the basis of fundamental principles, but making them relevant to the needs of concrete situations. His discipline contains and continues to develop such principles. His is not a trial-and-error trade. But neither is he, as professional man, a scholar or scientist or laboratory man (although he may be those things too as an individual). His job is mediating the principles to the needs of people in concrete situations. He is equally attentive to the principles and to the people.

2. He uses technical means that usually require a long time for mastery; but he uses them, rather than having them dictate to him. The minister's technical means may include the biblical languages, knowledge of how to counsel, and a grasp of group leadership or curriculum materials. The range is wide. And his mastery of them may fall short of virtuosity. But he uses them as the situation warrants. He is not enslaved to them individually or collectively, so that he must always use them whether relevant or not.

3. He is explicit to himself and others about a principle of limitation of function and responsibility. When someone in his own or another profession is prepared better than he to perform a service, he refers as soon as he can—and does not wait until he has tried everything and is at the end of his rope. With all developing professions, the limitation is not fixed but fluid. Nevertheless, it exists and is made explicit.

4. He operates in some fairly clear way in the direction of human welfare. This is obvious with physician and minister; but it is also true of the architect who, if he is professionally responsible, designs the houses in terms of his best understanding of

the people and their entire situation. Much human activity that turns out to be important proceeds otherwise, like the work of the laboratory scientist. The professional man, however, always has direct human welfare in mind.

5. He operates, finally, as a representative of a group that has some kind of ethics to govern its services to people who need them. Whether his is an old or a new profession, every act of professional responsibility that he undertakes is in the light of his professional ancestors and will affect his professional descendants, whether he realizes the fact or not. He is not alone.

If the minister is inattentive to any of these points, he is, however unwittingly, failing to exercise appropriate professional responsibility—or, in the context of this discussion, proper professional self-discipline. We may review the points with this in mind.

1. Basic principles related to concrete situations. New principles, or new understandings of principles, are being developed in theology no less than in the sciences. Is the minister, in some reasonable way, keeping up with them? Is he exploring and testing, and putting out for expert appraisal, his own ability to understand concrete situations and relating fundamental principles to them? If so, he is exercising on this point professional self-discipline.

2. Technical means mastered but not controlling. Is the minister keeping up with the developing technical means, or does he scorn all considerations of technique as unnatural? Or is he, in contrast, so bound to his technical methods that they blind him to the novelties in the situations he confronts? Is he afraid of a discussion after a speech, or of a speech before a discussion? Or does he keep after improving those elements of his technique where he is weak, while being, not unjustifiably, proud of those where he is strong? Does he simply favor his special skills, or does he also work at improving the others?

3. Acknowledging limitation. For the minister, this is no easy way out of the functions one does not like. It does mean disclaiming omniscience about what one likes and assuming responsibility for what one does not if it is essential to ministry. It means playing fair with those more skilled in various ways even if one does not approve all their views. Perhaps above all, it means

179

acknowledging that there are many people in the church who know a lot more about many things than the minister does.

4. Working directly for human welfare. Unless the minister believes that his supervisory work is as important as his direct service to persons, he will distort the meaning of this principle. He needs to believe that administering is as relevant to human welfare as preaching, and teaching as relevant as pastoral care, and so on. What he cannot do is to retreat to some ivory tower of routine without continuing to appraise the human welfare significance of what he is doing.

5. Representing his whole profession ethically. The minister, like any Christian, tries to represent Christ and the church. But in a more limited sense the minister always represents all ministers. Every act of his affects them, and he should be aware of this fact. Every act of his affects the shape of the entire ordained ministry. He may criticize his brethren, living or dead; but he does so in respect of his profession to which they also were and are committed.

I am sure that the shape of professional self-disciplining could be put in many other ways. This fashion has been especially helpful to me.

Disciplining Others: In Faith

Not only are heresy trials almost extinct, as they should be. Almost as dead are any real qualifications of belief and faith—so long as one keeps his mouth shut and does not talk manifest heresy. Every minister knows that a large number of his people could not pass any reasonable creedal test if it were put in fresh language and thought forms, even if they would assent to old statements they have interpreted in their own way.

It is possible and likely that most ministers, in a previous generation or century, interpreted the disciplining of their parishioners' faith as correcting them at least verbally. And we can hardly deny that in some quarters this is still the fashion. Most ministers, however, have swung to something near the opposite extreme. Nobody is ever corrected about anything. Discussion groups about matters of faith emphasize that everybody's view is wanted and welcome. Surely there is merit in this movement up to a point.

But it has limitations. Suppose that Mr. Jones is saying that of course God made the soul immortal and the Bible proves it. Since the Bible says no such thing, and the minister knows it, what does he do or say after first trying to understand Mr. Jones's meaning and accepting Mr. Jones as a person? These days he is likely to say almost nothing, and pass on to the next commentator lest he become "tangled" with Mr. Jones. I thoroughly disapprove of this procedure. This is an instance of golden opportunity to do noncoercive, democratic, but authoritative disciplining about the nature of the faith.

He does not have to be either gauche or rejecting in his procedure. He may well begin, "As I get your point, Mr. Jones, you believe such and such. The value of this to you is, I would guess from what you have said, such and such. And I like the value. But the fact is that the Bible does not support the basis upon which . . ." Let him, if necessary, tangle with Mr. Jones. Decently and in order, and careful to keep before himself constantly the distinction between respect for the person and acquiescence in misguided views.

Faith is not strictly a private affair in the sense that anybody's views are just as authoritative as those of anyone else. The early Protestant understanding of ministry was partly a tribute to this common sense. Today the minister is afraid that Mr. Jones may never come back if anything he says about faith is ever questioned. This kind of passive procedure eventually leads to two things. First, people come to think that it does not matter what you believe so long as you believe it sincerely, which is of course nonsense. Second, people come to think that faith is something you express a little bit on the proper occasion, but not something you reflect on and study and work on. It is this kind of attitude that tends to detheologize church discussions.

The good thing about the modern movement is that the person is not clobbered if he does not at once quote the right answer from the catechism. In principle, he has freedom to think and inquire for himself. But if there is no disciplining of the results of his inquiry—only, "It's fine that you are giving thought to

181

these matters"—then Christian faith is put in the realm of whim or fancy, and secret approval is given to the notion that anything goes if you believe it sincerely.

Faith is not merely right answers. Faith is indeed the process of inquiry, regardless of the status of the beliefs at any stage in the process. But the whole movement of faith is no more helped by approval of the effort than it is by rejective and merely technical corrections. If the minister is genuine about his respect for the person and his views no matter what they are, he will not harm the relationship if he appropriately disciplines the views.

I recall vividly an incident that occurred a dozen years or so ago, when I was conducting a series of meetings on a university campus. These had included some sessions for interested faculty members. Our procedure had been structured but informal, and there was free-swinging discussion at every stage. Justifiably prominent in the discussion was one professor who clearly and effectively disagreed with some of my views. In reply to him, I tried to state as clearly as possible what my views were and on what bases they rested. Finally he said something like this: "I still don't agree with you. But I want to congratulate you for not trying to pull aces out of your sleeve." I treasure that statement as one of the greatest compliments I have ever received, and I hope it was justified. He meant that I had stuck to my guns on my views, but had equally tried to understand his position. This story, in retrospect, is a reminder to me that disciplining is never without self-disciplining. I did indeed listen to the professor and his views, and learned something from them and him. He disciplined me just as I did him. And to our mutual profit, I believe.

Disciplining Others: In Life

At least until recent date there was a radical distinction between what one believed (if he was unobtrusive about it) and what he did. Most of the actual heresy trials, without judge and jury, were about matters of personal morals. If you were a Methodist minister, you had sworn not to touch alcohol, and you were not supposed to help anybody who did. If you were an Episcopalian, you could not remarry someone who had been divorced save

under such conditions that hardly anyone asked you; but if someone in this position showed up new in your parish, you knew it
would not be gentlemanly to throw him out. Every group, including my own, has had its idiosyncrasies about discipline in the
Christian life.

In the sense of "control over," not even the Roman Catholic
Church any longer has a power of discipline except through ex-
cluding offenders from its benefits. And it is not very happy with
such power. Protestantism tends to disclaim any desire for such
power in a "Good Joe" spirit, which means that it gets worked
up and angry when certain events occur and people are not "nice"
or "decent." A competent thief in his right mind will steal from
any source except a church.

Whatever disciplining behavior may mean these days on the
part of churches, there are no possible powers except exclusion
from the particular group (which, in a heterogeneous society, is
not being made a pariah) and possibly influencing public opinion.
What can disciplining of conduct mean, then, if it has no power
but persuasion (since exclusion is not the real issue)?

Generally speaking, what all this says to the minister's task is:
You can discipline life only through encouraging self-discipline.
Whether you can get to teen-agers or not, you have finally no
other resource than understanding and persuasion—no matter if
they use the pill, get pregnant, smoke marihuana, or become
delinquent. There is no "big stick." Quit kidding yourself.

In some degree there is more chance of creating power to
discipline life in adults. You may, if you like, get this or that person out of the church—like the homosexual person who is generally in control of himself but who has occasional relapses. But
what thank have ye on such points of decision?

The aim of the minister's disciplining others in life is precisely
as Joseph Fletcher has put it: teaching people to use the ultimate
criterion of love in the actual situation in making their decisions.
In the context of the present discussion, the same point could
be posed as helping people to discipline themselves in such a
direction that love is increasingly the criterion of their decisions.

PART III

The Integrity
of the Ministry

12
New Forms of Ministry

With new vigor in the early nineteenth century, the churches of Western Christendom, through the overseas missionary movement, began their long and ever more complex recognition that the ministry and church must go to people in special settings or with special problems. No matter that even in our own complex and secular day, when the old notion of "parish" as a particular area where people sleep and work has almost expired, the majority of people can still be ministered to by local churches for most of their lives if they are interested in the services of ministry. For some periods of his life however—college years, armed services, and the like—every person today needs a special ministry. And some people need special ministries most of their lives if they are to have any at all.

Following overseas missions, and then domestic missions to persons like the Indians, the next moves for special ministries were in the armed forces and in prisons. In those settings it was clear that men could be reached only through what became known as "chaplaincy" service, i.e., by special ministers able to be with them in their own settings. In the armed forces the decision was made early to make chaplains commissioned officers but to keep them "out of the line"; that is, to enable them to have a free relationship with the men they served. As time went on, the denominations had more to say about nominating their men (now an annual recertification is required); but the armed services rightly insisted on basic minimum qualifications of competence such as college and seminary experience and evidence of ability to do the job.

Even today an occasional church leader or group will declare that military chaplains are creatures of the military establishment. No such leaders, however, have tried to raise the millions that would be needed if the churches were to support their own chaplains financially. And to most observers it seems dubious whether the chaplains could have appropriate access to the men unless they are in uniform. The present system is one of careful checks and balances, with a great deal of sensitive attention to the proper protections of the chaplain as a church representative.

The history of ministry to men in prison is quite different. Until a quarter century ago such service was on two kinds of bases. First, there was a very small group of full-time chaplains, ordinarily getting their jobs because they were friends of the warden. When conscientious, as they often were, they found little time for actual ministry since so many obtrusive needs of a welfare nature caught their attention. Such men became, under the chaplaincy title, general welfare officers. Chaplains became free for ministry only when social workers, librarians, physicians, psychologists and other professional personnel became commonplace in our prisons just a few years ago.

The great majority of such institutions were served, however, only by part-time or visiting chaplains, with services often limited to the conduct of worship and funerals. Thus, even though prisons were among the first places of special need to catch the eye of the churches, it is only in the past quarter-century that the plan of full-time and specially trained chaplains, responsibly related to their churches as well as to their jobs, has become widespread. As in relation to the armed forces, it is now plain that the churches would be unready or unwilling to support financially an appropriate chaplaincy service; and that, even if they could or did, they might make it more difficult for their ministers to reach the men in their own settings.

It seems significant that, in these two settings where it became clear that the special situation demanded special ministry, the solutions finally worked out involved negotiated protection by the church of the actual ministry, but a budget from somewhere else. Although I do not wish to make a fetish of this principle, I believe that satisfactory negotiated solutions in the future on the part of many of the now emerging forms of ministry are very likely to follow a similar course. We shall do well to continue to cherish an appropriate respect for a sensibly interpreted separation of church and state in this country. And we may continue to criticize the partially state-supported churches of other parts of the world. But unless I misread the situation through too broad a generalization, I see our own churches simply reversing the place where nonchurch money goes; namely, ours goes into new ministries while our church money keeps store, while in some other parts of Christendom church money does the new projects and nonchurch money keeps store.

Ministry to the Sick

From here on, no attempt is made to distinguish the chronology of the churches' interest in one or another setting requiring special ministry. Ministry to the sick comes at this point in the discussion simply because I know more about it.

Thanks to the genius of Anton T. Boisen, the first mental hospital chaplain with special training for his job and founder of the movement for clinical education of the clergy, the first real advance in ministry to the sick came in the then unlikely field of public mental hospitals. Boisen began his work about 1924. He believed that mental patients were people and could often profit from a discriminating ministry if the chaplain understood them and their condition and potentialities. It is now almost the rule for public mental hospitals to have full-time chaplains who are regular members of the staff, and who are free to perform ministry along the patterns carved out in the armed forces and penal institutions. Private mental hospitals, of which there are only a few, have been slower to follow this trend. Again, it may be noted that very little church money is involved in ministry within mental hospitals.

Ministry in the general hospital was first approached in a radically new way by Russell L. Dicks in Boston. His work too was a project of the Boisen movement for clinical education of the clergy. Because general hospitals, unlike most mental hospitals, were under many kinds of administrative auspices (churches, community funds, self-perpetuating boards, as well as public agencies), the advance in chaplaincy service within them has had to take a variety of financial patterns. What has given unity to ministry in general hospitals has been the increasing insistence that the men have special and supervised clinical education in preparation for their work.

The case of chaplaincy in church hospitals is worth a special note. When the chaplaincy movement got underway in its modern form in the 1930's, there were about 450 hospitals affiliated with Protestant churches, whether loosely or tightly. Only a handful of these had full-time chaplains, virtually none with special training for his work. Many of them, however, had superintendents or administrators who were ministers and were also supposed to serve as chaplains. In the interim period most of these ordained minister-administrator-chaplains have been replaced, on the one side, by trained hospital administrators, and on the other side by trained chaplains. For the most part, Protestant hospitals today do provide economic support for their chaplains. But of course few such hospitals could keep operating if they did not continue to accept tax funds for various kinds of needs, including new buildings. Indeed, it is doubtful if any Protestant-related hospitals today could give adequate support of their chaplains if new sources of income (including things like Blue Cross but also, above all, tax money) had not become available to them.

It is curious, however, and a bit disconcerting, to find that the chaplaincy principle in relation to the sick has won its way most solidly and convincingly at just those points where the "institutional" elements are most solid and even rigid, and has been least successful in those settings where health and medical care is being taken to the people. Even in clinics for out-patient care in connection with general or mental hospitals, there have been few attempts to include religious ministry among the available services; whereas the chaplaincy service to the bed patients in the same institution may be excellent. For the most part, the same thing is true of the health and welfare services that operate mostly through "offices" such as family and child-care agencies, public or private. Catholic agencies have sometimes made a stab at including priests,

190

but usually only for special "moral" services or as regular social case workers.

The new challenge that is upon us relates first to the emerging large number of community mental health centers, and eventually to the perhaps even more important general community health centers. To qualify for federal money each such center must agree to offer a range of services by no means confined to bed treatment, and must make them available to all persons in a district who need and want them. Thus treatment, early detection, prevention, and education are all combined in some proportion.

This movement is developing so rapidly that no one has yet been able to study comprehensively the relationship of clergymen to it. Several centers are known where there are chaplains, or church-liaison officers, or clergymen with similar titles. But no one can yet know what direction this movement should take so far as the ordained ministry is concerned. Clearly there must be some kind of liaison, including education of the clergy in the area. Also clearly there must be some kind of special ministry to those persons who cannot receive it from a local church clergyman. But how and in what proportions? And what shall the churches do about those centers that carry an antipathy to any expert service of ministry? This is one of the genuine pioneering areas of our time for vital ministry precisely to those in great need. It may be even more so when, as is true in many instances, these community health centers serve disadvantaged populations of various kinds.

I am strongly inclined to believe that the chaplaincy model, at least as developed up to the present time in hospitals, prisons, and the armed forces, is not adequate to guide the new development with the health centers. Its emphasis on genuinely understanding the person is all to the good, as is its insistence on high standards of education for ministry. But it is accustomed to having people in bed or "around." The looser setting of the health center requires a great many more forays into the highways and byways. If the chaplaincy model can so adapt itself, well and good. If not, a new model will have to be found.

Our society moves very slowly to improve or create agencies to deal with various special kinds of sickness or handicap. At long last, thanks especially to John F. Kennedy, some progress is being made in relation to the mentally retarded. The treatment of some of these persons will continue to require institutions, hopefully much improved institutions, where ministry can be brought through our present chaplaincy model. But we now know that, with proper appraisal from every relevant side and proper guidance, a very large proportion of mentally deficient persons can live either in their own homes or in foster homes. How can the special guidance also include, where appropriate, religious ministry? We are only on the threshold of exploring this question.

About two years ago, and for the first time, the federal government through the National Institutes of Health set up a special fund concerned with the care and treatment of alcoholic persons. The states have been moving into this area, but slowly and cautiously. Far too many alcoholics are left with no resources at all unless they happen to be candidates for Alcoholics Anonymous, whose program is suitable for only a certain proportion. For helping many alcoholics, I am convinced that we shall need far more multilevel institutions that serve only alcoholics (through bed care, day-hospital care, out-patient care, etc.) as well as an increase in facilities that are part of general and mental hospitals and other kinds of institutions.

Of the very few existing multilevel institutions that serve alcoholic patients, the most notable experimentation with chaplaincy service has been at the Georgian Clinic in Atlanta. Its program of service and ministry has demonstrated that the clergy can be trained for a special ministry to alcoholics, provided there are more institutions that can use their services as active members of the staff cooperating with others. The staffing pattern of a good alcohol center, however, must be in part different from that of either the mental or the general hospital.

There have been some experiments in ministry to those who are physically severely handicapped, but our knowledge in this area is still in its infancy. For a number of years a succession of my ministerial graduate students served as part-time chaplains at the Illinois Children's Hospital School, much to my own benefit in terms of learning. Both the pathos and the courage of many such children, suffering appalling handicaps and sometimes with the certain knowledge of imminent death, was for me a kind of trek with Job. Certainly the future should see a few ministers with full competence to minister in these tragic but often subtly rewarding situations.

But there are other kinds of opportunities for ministry to those handicapped in various ways. Today our general services to handicapped persons are very much fragmented. There seem to be special services for almost every kind of handicap—blindness, deafness, lost limbs, and so on. As the general "rehabilitation" concept catches on, as I believe it must, there may be opportunity for ministry side by side with experts in various kinds of handicap rehabilitation. What such ministry might just possibly accomplish in specific cases could be as significant as the technical help that is also needed. So far, most of this is crystal-gazing, but I believe it will come.

The baffling subject of the various kinds of drug addiction and use has, finally, been lifted out of the dark corners and become an object of public and church concern. Not much more than ten years ago a competent student of mine at the University of Chicago who had done good experimental work trying to help addicts wrote his B. D. essay on this subject. At that time, despite my best efforts and his, we could not find a publisher. One publisher told us that the subject was not of sufficient general interest.

How our society will proceed in relation to drugs and addictions is plainly moot at the present time. Some of the free-floating experimental centers run by ministers seem to be doing good work. In the long run, however, science and medicine will properly be in charge of much of this work, and ministry will have to be conducted through staff cooperation just as in relation to physical and mental illness, alcoholism, and other health problems. A few expert ministers preparing for such service will be of use.

In mentioning, in this section on the sick, some kinds of sex problems including some forms of homosexuality, I do not want to imply that all sex problems, or all homosexuality, are simply to be categorized as "sickness." Happily, the National Institute of Mental Health will soon be considering the establishment of a research institute on those sexual problems that properly fall under the health heading. But they rightly realize, for instance, that except for their aberration many homosexual persons are not mentally unhealthy. Now that Kinsey and his associates, and subsequently others like Johnson and Masters, have courageously brought research about sex problems into public view, it is very likely that a few expert ministers equipped to work along with clinicians will be needed in the future.

This brief discussion of various forms of sickness and of the settings in which they may be treated, cared for, alleviated, or prevented is very far from being exhaustive. The general conclusion is, however, that a small number of specially trained ministers will be needed much more in the near future than in the past, and that the chaplaincy model helps with most of these up to a point but must be supplemented and altered if some of the most genuine needs are to be met.

Ministry to the Disadvantaged

Up to this point the discussion has been about kinds of needs of persons and types of settings where they can be helped with which I have long familiarity. The present section finds me, however, no more expert than the next person. The brevity and caution of the material is the confession of my ignorance. But the presence of this section at all is simply a tribute to its nearly overwhelming social importance today.

From my reading over several years of the excellent East Harlem Protestant Parish reports, the initial experimental ministry of its kind, I have drawn two general conclusions. The first is that the relative success has been a judicious mixture, on the part of the staff, of genuine empathy with the people they serve in every aspect of their lives along with imaginative and resourceful evocation of the leadership potentials in the people. The second is that, when applied relevantly but often unconventionally, it is the traditional tools of ministry, and not mere gimmicks or "forgetting" Christian faith and worship, that have brought most lasting returns. Since chaplaincies in general have also been successful to the degree that they have discovered the same two principles I have often wished that East Harlem (and other projects like it in Chicago and elsewhere) and the chaplaincy leaders could get together. There is more that is worthy of mutual exchange than either seems to have realized to date. So far, there has been little such exchange.

The urban centers, however they are organized (by existing local churches, by roving ministers, etc.) and regardless of their auspices (church, community, or what), are immediately in the midst of problems of race, poverty, delinquency, mental illness in children and adults, and much else. Even if we temporarily think of this ministry as rehabilitative service to the persons and families caught in their individual situations, and for the moment set aside the social action aspects needed to provide them collectively with a new base of operations, our ignorance about how to proceed is formidable. Mental illness and alcoholism and similar problems may be just as bad, but they tend to provide specific targets. The appalling fact about ministry in today's inner city is that there are so many targets one must try to hit all at once.

There seem to me to be three general kinds of temptation faced by ministers working in our inner cities today, apart from graft and the lure of the suburbs. The first is a "Holy Grail" conception of their function, not unlike that of the early overseas Christian missionaries of the past century. The trouble with this model is that, in the face of the complex situations and their long history, it invites disillusionment and retreat. When a minister is paid, or underpaid, by his church, he may flirt even more with this temptation. By eventually refusing to cooperate with local "social workers," who seem to him to be of the Establishment, he may actually be declaring, in defensive fashion, that nobody but a Christian minister can get on with the job—that there are no men of goodwill if they get decently paid and are frequently baffled about what to do next.

The second temptation is so to emphasize the social action route that the ministry of service to persons and families is either neglected or regarded only as a palliative. All this is very human. When the problems are added up, they do indeed appear so overwhelming that nothing but "basic social change" seems to be the answer. Ambulances seem to become parts of the Establishment rather than aspects of the answer. And yet I believe there can

195

be no ministry that dispenses with ambulances, although a ministry confining itself to them would be halfhearted and foreshortened.

The third temptation is to become so immersed in the local situation that the aims of ministry itself may be forgotten. The plight of many people and families is so deep and complex and interwoven, and serious attempts to help make it ever more clear that outsiders do not really understand. The resulting temptation, in the case of ministers, is to believe that what the church and churchmen stand for cannot have much relevance to the situation.

In the early days of chaplaincy service and clinical pastoral education, something very like this turned out for a while to be the main temptation. Clinical students, spending hours writing up a pastoral call so that it could be analyzed—and seeing the immense complexities in the person and relationship—were startled by the breezy minister from outside the hospital who rolled in, issued a few exhortations and a prayer, and departed happy that he had done his stint. What the movement of course had to do, and did subsequently get round to doing, was to assume leadership responsibility for helping the breezy minister to learn better how to do his job. As in the present situation, however, the temptation at first was to treat this kind of ministry as so new and different that it was not to be thought of as ministry in the traditional sense at all.

The churches have happily been able to do some pioneering in urban centers, which of course needs to be continued. As such a center works its way into the lives and needs of disadvantaged peoples, however, more and more expert persons are brought into the picture in some capacity—health center personnel, social agency workers, persons who can find jobs, vocational training teachers, and many others. The social patterns for organizing such services are still confused almost to the point of chaos. But if needs are to be met except in some token or pilot project fashion, it seems clear that the churches are no more inherently equipped to be general administrators of such programs utilizing all relevant resources than they would be to run our mental hospitals and community mental health centers. An urban center under church auspices that succeeds in getting personnel to offer

196

the needed variety of services will no doubt survive, in just the same way that our church-related hospitals have survived. But with church resources as limited as they are, and the need so great, it seems clear that the churches will have to develop patterns of working alongside other personnel, with the chief resources coming from elsewhere than the churches and with administrative patterns different from those in which the minister is also the general administrator. At this point I hope that the Holy Grail temptation will yield to visions of the new service that secular administration and financing can bring—without losing sight of the need to have a dimension of ministry involved on the team.

I know even less about rural than urban centers, but I am sure the details of such programs will be different. There has been some bold experimentation by the churches in certain depressed areas—for instance, in the Appalachians. There are increasing signs that here also church programs will not have to go it alone. Ministry may cooperate with new and welcome allies. But it ought to preserve the dimension of ministry even if the overall job is being done largely by others.

Regardless of location—urban, rural, suburbs, or the megalopolis no-man's-land—there are disadvantaged persons who need the concern and ministry of the church both in social action to help get new bases and also in terms of immediate needs now. Some delinquents can be helped before they get to reform school. Some criminals, even if they have served time, can be helped by ministry not to go back to old ways. What the churches and YMCA's and settlement houses have already been doing for disadvantaged teen-agers ought not to be overlooked; but there can be more of it, better planning, wider coverage, and new methods.

A very large proportion of the older people in this country are still disadvantaged despite the major steps of old-age and survivors' federal insurance and, more recently, of Medicare. It must, of course, be remembered that there is no necessary psychological disadvantage in the process of growing older. Many older people are as active within the limits of their strength as younger people, as happy and contributive to society. But there is a kind of underground bias against them as a group on the part of the dominant middle-years population. This fact was brought home

197

to me a year ago in one of the far-western states. A large retirement housing project had been built on the edge of a relatively small city. According to my informants, it was well planned—an apartment complex rather than a dormitory-type institution. The appalling fact the local ministers confronted was that their parishioners would not accept these new older people into the life and work of the congregations. I gave the ministers encouragement. But it may well be that special ministry will eventually have to come. The virulence of the segregation motif seemed great.

Many ministers today are sufficiently alert to the problems confronted after retirement to be available to their people to counsel on such matters at the proper time. But it now seems high time that society (and I do not know which professional group should assume the central responsibility) should have interprofessional counseling teams to help people at this juncture in their lives, especially for the disadvantaged but also for others. If this development comes as it should, then we shall need a few specially trained ministers to work with retirement counseling teams.

At the other end of the age scale there are the children in trouble. Such children are disadvantaged whatever the income of their parents and whether their trouble is defined as mental illness or something else. Currently a nation-wide study of the mental health of children is in progress, and it plans to include a good many of the problems and needs of troubled children beyond clear-cut mental illness. Since the treatment facilities for troubled children are, everywhere, woefully inadequate, the report will no doubt recommend the creation of many others. We shall need a few ministers with special knowledge capable of working along these lines. In my consultative work I have nowhere been more baffled than when asked what a center for disturbed children could do about ministry. Things can indeed be done. But only a very unusual kind of minister can do them.

With some hesitation lest a successful Amazon somewhere accuse me of calling her names, I nevertheless include in this roster of disadvantaged persons many single women—unmarried, widowed, or divorced. To say that most such women are doing well and are not Amazons is entirely true. Yet the attitudes of our society, family oriented as we are, are such that an attribution of disadvantage—thus making the lot harder than it should be—is the rule rather than the exception. One of my former students, an able woman minister, is currently engaged in an experimental ministry to such women living in apartment hotels. Some of her stories are almost as gruesome for their loneliness as anything coming from the mental hospital or the slums. Here also, some few expert ministers are likely to be needed in the future—along with aiding all ministers to be sensitive to the special needs here that are created by the cryptically rejecting attitudes of a family-oriented society.

This account is very far from exhausting the complexity of disadvantaged persons in our society. But it does attempt to lift up the most obvious, and also the most neglected, disadvantaged groups. Pioneering ministries are going on with many of these groups, and pioneering will always be needed as new problems come into public view. But a sensible society that can afford it— and we can—will in due course set up integrated and multipro-fessional resources to help with many of these problems. Eventually, therefore, the ministry of the church will be cooperative in these areas with the patterns set up by society to deal with them. We need to think even now of making this transition. What the church should hang on to is not particular programs and institutions but the conviction that, in the meeting of any special need, there is a legitimate place for ministry as a co-operating dimension of service.

New-Form Ministries in Old Settings

More of our local churches are growing larger, and the phe-nomenon of multiple-staff ministry has come upon many of them unaware. We are only on the threshold of finding out how one learns to be a "senior minister," or what, in addition to his area of professional expertness, any other staff member needs to know and do to contribute to the total service of the ministerial staff. Studies that include secretaries, sextons, architects, business man-agers, lay counselors, and other nonordained local church staff personnel are almost nonexistent. Nobody says anything analytical about church music in terms of its administrative coherence within the church. So far as I have any key to this new kind of "collegiate" ministry, it is given in the previous chapter on administering. Just as any minister needs to realize in a new degree that the ministry he is to get done is to be done largely through other people and in consultation with them, so the ministers in multiple-staff situations need to go even a step further—and realize that the principle applies first among themselves and also to their lay co-workers. Nothing namby-pamby about either authority or responsibility—but a final forsaking of the lone-wolf image of ministry.

Ever since I heard of campus ministry and was involved in it at the start of my own work, such ministries have been in crisis. Indeed, the heresy among campus ministers is when one says he knows how to do it. There are good reasons for this high degree of professional self-criticism in campus ministry. One is the obvious time limit one has to perform it, for a campus is a community that knows, at the time it comes, when it is getting out. Psychologically, most of its members are not putting down roots. It is harder to minister to people who still oil the wheels on their trailers.

But more important are the changing patterns and attitudes of campus life, the enormously increased and still increasing numbers of young people who are on campuses, and the various kinds of movements that combine to make young people think of religion and the church as false, traditional, or irrelevant. Against all these trends, however, is the still continuing increase in solid academic courses about religious matters, even in tax-supported institutions.

As to what the new forms in campus ministry are or should be, I confess myself as baffled as most of the competent campus ministers I know. As a result of running an experimental course at the University of Chicago for two years, for those preparing for campus ministries, in which we focused on personal service and pastoral care to students, I am convinced that more insight and skill in this area could be of great benefit to campus ministers, most of whom currently perform these functions without special training. I am convinced too that a Ph.D., or whatever else aids the campus minister to be respected by the faculty, provides new

200

opportunities. And the evidence of social relevance, even in the style of William Sloane Coffin, Jr., has its points. But for an over-all solution we shall have to await some genuinely inspired campus minister who can do our theoretical work for us. Nevertheless, new forms are clearly needed.

Another new form of ministry, mostly exercised in an old setting, is the pastoral counseling center. Here one or more ministers, with special education in pastoral counseling, give service to individual persons and families according to their need. To date, most such centers are under the auspices of either a local church, a group of such churches, or a local council of churches. This kind of organization of service may be of genuine value not only to members of local churches but also to others who, while sympathetic to religion or the church, have nevertheless not gone so far as to join a church. In a very indirect but often significant way, help by the church may mean later a new look at it. Hence, these centers may be, unobtrusively, effective agents of evangelism. A competent center makes sure that it has medical, psychiatric, and psychological consultants or staff members, even though its principal work is done by ministers.

Some such centers have gone independent, and a few are in or near the quackery line, simply exploiting the interest but neither meeting the standards of competence nor relating themselves appropriately to the church in an administrative sense. A new group called the American Association of Pastoral Counselors is attempting to certify the abilities of individual ministers and also to accredit the counseling centers. Although I have been critical of some aspects of its work to date, it is clear that functions of this kind are needed.

The temptation of the minister who has qualified himself in pastoral counseling relates to money. If he so chooses and his denomination does not reprimand him, he may elect to "free-lance" either full-time (by creating a center that permits him to receive fees directly) or part-time (by working part of his time in a legitimate center that pays him a salary but does not forbid him to take fees from individuals for other hours).

As a minister, one represents the church in some significant way and cannot be merely a free-lance. The main point of principle is that no one should be deprived of his services through financial considerations alone. A sliding scale will of course help. But the final and necessary guarantee that he represents the church, administratively speaking, is that some proper corporate body (and not individuals who are served) gives him his money. To do otherwise is to risk in this area, as Wayne E. Oates has rightly noted, the same kind of situation the churches got into with free-lance evangelists.

I have asked the American Association of Pastoral Counselors to include a provision that receiving direct fees from persons for personal services be sufficient reason to withhold certification of the minister as a pastoral counselor. So far, the Association has shown no inclination to take such action. At the present time, therefore, the policing agent on this crucial point must be the specialist minister himself and his own conception of the representative nature of the ministry.

Still thinking of new forms of ministry in old settings, I find myself both encouraged and distressed by the overseas opportunities and situations. My special studies in this area have been on mission hospitals and clinics. Some very good new planning is going on about relating Christian medical institutions overseas to the rapidly advancing indigenous health services. Yet far too little attention has been given to updating religious ministry in relation to these institutions, regardless of who pays their bills. For instance, in India at one of the two major Christian medical centers, where the senior chaplain has several associates, no provision is made either in India or the United States for this chaplain to advance his training either in chaplaincy or in supervision. For our mission boards to take such needs seriously seems to me an elementary conclusion. But it still remains to be done.

Some recent contact with the overseas arm of my own church was generally reassuring about the program shifts required in our new age. But the Holy Grail, although a little tarnished, still seemed far too much in evidence. Most overseas programs are deeply involved in education, medical care, and even agriculture, and have competent specialists to work on these areas. But is the "ministry" that goes along with them still "evangelistic" in the old missionary sense, i.e., actually uneducated in a pastoral sense

202

and not properly connected with the other dimensions of mission? Frankly, I am not much reassured by what I know of the answer. That Holy Grail is the bugaboo.

There are many other new forms of ministry going on these days within old settings. There are imaginative programs for teen-agers and young people, significant programs of camping and retreat, many imaginative racial programs, programs that involve guidance about occupations, programs in schools of various kinds, and many others. My list is surely not exhaustive.

There are also some new programs of ministry to ministers—counseling with the help sometimes of psychological testing instruments, but designed to focus on vocation and career and not merely upon problems that should better be dealt with by psychiatrists. It seems clear that this special kind of counseling ministry to ministers will increase, and that more specially trained ministers will be needed to man it.

New-Form Ministries in New Settings

Under the general principle that the church should go to the people, so far as possible, wherever they are, I have tried to think of new settings to which ministry has been recently taken. Perhaps I have become an old-timer, but the fact is that most of the "new settings" I can think of were long since thought of by imaginative churchmen who did something about it.

The ministry to migrant workers has been going on for forty or fifty years. Ministries to persons, urban and rural, who can manage only some language other than English are at least as old. Ministries on the Indian reservations are very old. Those to visitors to our national parks are now approaching antiquity. To be sure, even in these old-timers, new methods can make great improvements in old ministries. But whatever the quality of program, which has often been mixed, the churches have been alert to new settings of need.

Just after World War II, I was much involved in trying to get "industrial chaplaincy" going. Under the principle of availability to men in their work setting, we thought there might be a new chaplaincy opportunity finally as significant as what we had discovered in hospitals, prisons, and the armed forces. We had no objection to industry's paying a good part of the bill so long as organized labor equally approved the notion and contributed at least something to prove it. Our hopes were subsequently shown to be false. I am sure that there are still a few industrial chaplains who perform competent service and are not wholly captive to their industries. But we never got labor organizations to contribute any more than the churches; and indeed, in this financial respect, they may in fact be quite similar. Failing this, it is a blessing that we have had no great crusade for industrial chaplains.

At last report, one of my former students was Protestant chaplain of the Chicago Police Department and taking his job as full-time and very active, not merely blessing picnics or special events. Perhaps there could be more of a future here, if only he would analyze his experience in writing for us. Because we still have hangovers from past days, all kinds of voluntary organizations, or even sometimes public groups, in the community have their *pro-forma* "chaplains." In our curious twilight zone between a Christian culture and a secularized society these positions are likely to be looked at askance by the intelligentsia and by church people alike. They may indeed be marks of Religion on the Potomac. But if any minister ever takes seriously the opportunities for ministry, as did my student with the Chicago police, then I think something entirely different happens. Taken seriously, such posts may help both persons and policy in a significant way.

No doubt there are many other new settings in which ministry is being assayed of which I am ignorant. Let me comment, however, on those ministers who conceive their calling to be working with "revolutionary" groups of all kinds. This may be the revolution of black power, protest against the selective service, revolution of the arts (which have otherwise been neglected in this account), of sexual conduct, and the like. For the most part, such experimental ministries have begun ideologically, with a concern for certain kinds of social change. The question is: What do they do when they deal with live people who are revolutionary in relation to the particular issue? Are they simply comrades in arms, or are they also ministers? What troubles me is that the former, which may be very important, so often seems to drive out the latter.

Conclusion

While not denying that there are genuine new forms of ministry, including those in old settings and new, this chapter has mainly attempted to get at the principles of relationship involved in new thrusts or forms or settings of ministry. Heaven forbid that these should stop us from getting into new settings where we are needed, or from developing new methods that are vital or new forms that are more relevant and equally true to the gospel and church we represent.

But the fact remains, as a result of this analysis, that our immediate ministerial forebears were at least as imaginative as we are, that they saw many opportunities and went after them, with fewer resources than we have to meet them; and that some of the touted new forms are not so novel after all. Let us by no means stop novelty where it can better meet needs. But let us not be ignorant of a history of ministry that has had, for a long time, great sensitivity and imagination about what needs to be done, whatever its small resources in trying to meet the need.

Let me encourage any young or budding minister to follow his nose about new forms of ministry that excite him and that promise to bring the gospel to the needs of some needy section of mankind. But let me caution him against any conception of novelty that is based on ignorance of what our immediate ancestors have been up to.

13
The Unity of the Ministry

This is a picture-talk book. For every basic function of ministry there has been time to consider, I have either set forth the
explicit cartoon-like image of function or, in some instances when
history had not made such an image explicit, have constructed one
from the implicit meanings. But this is not a picture book.

At one point in my work I consulted my publisher to see if he
could find an artist who would draw cartoons for my images. The
wise answer was that he could—but would it help or hinder if we
got actual cartoons? To be sure, if we had them, the inattentive
reader might look at them just as he looks at the photographs in
Life. But if the purpose of my images is not to impede reading of
the text, but is instead to aid the reader to do his own thinking
more confidently in images (I think he does it anyhow), then
might not the pictorial gain be offset by apparently not appealing
to the reader's imagination? I believe my publisher is wise, and I
have followed his counsel. For, cartoons or no cartoons, imagination is required in seeing these images of the ministry and their
interrelationship.

Even before I began making the notes that have led to this
book, and long before I began writing it, I was convinced that the
ordained ministry is a unity, although a complex one, functionally
speaking. I was supposed to be a specialist in matters like pastoral
care. But I found myself riled when people assumed that this
specialism meant that I could not preach, made sure that I would
be a poor administrator, assumed me to be unconcerned about
getting the gospel to people, found me a psychologist instead of a

theologian, and took it for granted that I could never take a hard-nosed line because I supported people.

Had I been in a local church for most of my ministry, I suppose I should have done what has been done by my able and insightful friends who have followed that course; namely, worked it through personally and professionally, realized that the ministry is a unity, although one of complex functions, and from then on kept publicly quiet. It may be a legacy of my early commitment to a specialized form of the ministry that makes me try to articulate this and work it through and not simply take it for granted. It is also on the basis of my contact with hundreds of ministers, especially among the younger and more alert, that I decided to write this book. True, they must find out the complex unity of the ministry, finally, for themselves. But why should they not have a spot of help?

The Nine Images

When I began rediscovering or constructing the several images of ministerial functioning, I decided to reserve judgment on where —except individually—they would come out. No predetermined conclusion that they would emerge at a central point, no foreordained conviction that they would remain separate, seemed appropriate. Consequently, so far as was possible, I took up each function and its image as phenomenologically as possible. And of course all the time I knew that the nine types of function selected for consideration were not exhaustive of the ministry.

Let me remind the reader about the basic elements in the cartoon images as they emerged:

Preaching. The image includes the elements of preacher, open Bible, and pulpit. The Word of God comes through the Bible but is not equated with the Bible as book. The Bible rests on the pulpit, not on the preacher. The people are symbolically represented by the pulpit, and are uplifted as is the preacher in hearing the Word. The preacher has the same message, through the Word, for himself that he has for others. Although no explicit feedback arrangement is shown in the image, the authority of the minister's interpretation of the Word depends upon his dedication and competence and is not above question by those who hear.

Administering. The elements include one minister and at least two laymen, whatever their size, sex, or color. All are shown at the same level, whether standing or in another posture. All are looking in the same direction. The minister has a hand on the shoulder of each to demonstrate that his authority is encouragement plus skill. But only in concert can the functions of ministry be accomplished.

Teaching. The constructive image here includes a minister, perhaps also a second minister as special religious educator, a round table, several persons of different characteristics such as age, sex, and color, and some symbols on the table like Bible or cross. The teaching by the minister is in dialogue or trialogue. The symbols show it is not just any old kind of content but Christian content. The second minister, hopefully a woman, shows that the minister is teaching even when he is not exclusively in charge.

Shepherding. Both an old and a new model were offered to the reader. If he could stand sheep, we offered the picture of a minister or shepherd kneeling and taking the burrs off a particular sheep. But even with the ancient image updated, we warned that there should be a walkie-talkie beside him—and the implicit assurance that if the sheep was too sick for burr-control, a helicoptor would show up to take him to the vet. The modern version of the image, minus sheep, was presented as the minister at the hospital bedside—sitting down so he and the patient are at the same level, with something like a Bible or cross shown in the picture but manifestly not used as a weapon over the sufferer.

Evangelizing. The elements of this image are a minister, a group representing different fixed characteristics such as race or age, some symbols like Bible or cross to provide the context—and a translator. With persons ready to listen to the gospel, this is a good image. We were not able also to provide an image of those who just might hear it but are not now so inclined, except through showing quizzicality and belligerence in one or two of the group.

208

Celebrating. Taking the Communion or Lord's Supper as normative here, the image included table with the elements, minister, and supporting celebrants. Our analysis showed this one image as inadequate to cover all Christian celebrating. Still, it is clearly central.

Reconciling. The elements here were a minister with a gavel, a group, a table, and a Bible on the table. The gavel was discussed as the instrument of rational and accepted authority, not over but with. We noted that the reconciling process cannot begin until something like this fact is present, even though ministerial activity may have to make its efforts long before.

Theologizing. Here we had a minister in his study with some books, clearly including the Bible, an open window showing some symbols (like a factory) of the activity and confusion of modern society, and something like a typewriter to show the minister as an active scholar and not just a passive recipient. The first seven images show actual activities of ministry. This, and the one to follow, show preparation for activity. Or, to be more precise, they show that activity with others is meaningless unless there has first been activity with the professional self.

Disciplining. Here the minister is shown in an attitude of prayer, with appropriate symbols like Bible or prayer book—but with the whole before an open window which, like the image of theologizing, demonstrates the purpose of ministry to the world as it is.

Their Common Elements

Until I had analyzed each of these nine functional images individually and phenomenologically in detail, it had not occurred to me that in a general way they all have certain elements in common. There are of course also differences, some shown in the images themselves and others only appearing in the full photograph of the function. But the common elements in the images astonished me. Here they are.

1. Every image contains something like the Bible or the cross

to show that this context is unique, however much it may be like other situations in certain respects.

2. Every image has at least one minister (some more than one, as in teaching); but he is never alone if we read beyond the cartoon itself. Even the images that stress preparation rather than performance, theologizing and disciplining, imply a subsequent service relationship to people.

3. The minister is shown as accepting leadership, but interpreting this as putting him on the same level as the people except for his presumed competence and responsibility for coordination. Even in shepherding he kneels to help the sheep, or sits rather than stands at the bedside. In the pulpit he is raised; but so, symbolically, are the people—to hear the Word.

4. In some images explicitly, but in all implicitly, the ministry is to all sorts, ages, colors, sexes, and conditions and attitudes of men. In one or two of the images anxious, belligerent, or who-do-you-think-you-are expressions have been suggested. The minimum condition is that they are there and present. No gung ho required.

These common elements of the images seem enough to suggest to me that there must be some kind of unity to the ministry—even though, in the analysis of these restricted images, it is also plain that one cannot move literalistically from one image to another without allowing for context and specifics.

But preaching and evangelizing are not telling them without consulting them, our images show. Pastoral care is not being nice to them with the prospect of someday clobbering them through disciplining. Reconciling is not getting unanimity so that teaching in some artificial one-way sense is thereafter the order of the day. Theologizing is not getting it so ordered that nothing is left but dishing it out. And so on.

What our functional images point to is a unified attitude about ministry—complex enough to take various needs and functions and situations as they come, but with no sense of inherent contradiction among them. You thought you were simply engaged, shepherding fashion, in helping and encouraging Mrs. Sizzle. But when she goes on to criticizing the church, taking apart the book of Genesis, denigrating the morals of the clergy, and attacking the Communion service, why is it not both wise and fun to shift gears and deal with her on those terms? Only a complexly unified ministry can do this.

The Ambiguity of Unity

What are the "units" of a complex unity? At least in the ministry, they are not purely behavioral. We cannot say the unity lies in talk; so go on talking. But neither is it in listening alone, nor in performing traditional rites, nor in being attentive to the voice of the news, nor in hatchet-buryings between various kinds of antagonists.

Function is larger than behavior. Function always tries toward goals but with no necessary security that those goals can be reached. Christian function is bound to rely at times on certain traditional means, such as those of celebration and preaching. But beyond those, and within the limits of decency and order, it may use any means at hand to move a step ahead.

Its preparations are almost inseparable from its activities. Theologizing and disciplining may be seen as the images show them here, as preparation; but unless they issue in function, they are vain. By the same token, the other seven images that are shown in active function could have been shown, instead, in terms of preparation. For every function there is preparation, else the ministry is not responsible.

But unity contains ambiguity if it is the kind of unity that, in the mind of the minister, makes it hang together for him despite the variety of his activities seen in the usual categories. The ambiguity is deepened because the skills needed are very rarely present in high degree in any one person. But it seems to me it is just this ambiguity that adds to the zest of ministering, in any setting new or old. Forget the perfectionism; do well what you can do well; shore up your weaknesses to some point—and then rejoice that you are not on the assembly line doing the same thing every ten minutes. For those who want assembly lines, the ministry is the wrong place to look.

211

Index

Acceptance, in preaching and
pastoral counseling, 64-68
Administering, 69-85
as commitment through
group, 76-80
ministers' dislike of, 69-72
norm of, taken from pathologies, 75
normative image of, 76-80
pathologies of, 72-75
psychology of, 81-84
reasons for hating, by ministers, 81-84
theology of, 76-80
Advent, 42
Alcoholics, 192
America, ministry in Colonial,
38-39
American Association of Pastoral Counselors, 201, 202
American scholarships, as functionally oriented, 31-32
Anti-intellectualism
in America, 163
in the ministry, 29
Apologetics, 123
Appraisal
fear of in the ministry, 82-83
as teaching, 90
Aquinas, Thomas, 24
Arbitration, 156

Augustine, 168

Baptism, as celebrating, 141
Baptist farmer preachers, 38
Barth, Karl, 29, 40, 60, 70, 162,
167, 168, 169
Baxter, Richard, 87
Beeners, W. J., 10
Berkeley, George, 161
Bible, in preaching image, 53-56
Bishops, 33, 36, 37
Blake, Eugene Carson, 24
Blizzard, Samuel, 69
Boisen, Anton T., 189
Bone, Harry, 102
Bonhoeffer, Dietrich, 168
Boy Scouts, 83
Breakdown of ministers, 15, 19-
20
Brethren, Church of the, 141
Brite Divinity School, 9
British churches, 23, 38, 39
Brunner, Emil, 41, 168
Buddhism, 154
Bultmann, Rudolf, 40, 162, 168

Calvin, John, 51, 63, 86, 164
Campus ministry, 116-17, 200-
201
Cars, as ministerial castles, 75
Cartwright, Peter, 24, 161, 167

213

Gaseous analogy of preaching, 61-62
Gavel image, 146
General hospital chaplaincy, 189-90
Georgian Clinic, 192
Gestalt psychology, 83
Good Friday, 133
Graham, Billy, 113, 114
Group counseling image, 110

Handicapped, chaplaincy to, 192-93
Handshake image, 145-46
Harvard University, 93, 94, 116
Harvard University Divinity School, 21, 22
Heidegger, Martin, 70
Heidelberg Catechism, 71
Hemingway, Ernest, 70
"Higher" calling image, 93-94
Hinduism, 154
Hired-man image, 160-61
Hitler, Adolf, 156
Hobbies, 177
"Holy Grail" image, 195
Homosexuality, ministry in relation to, 193-94
Honest to God (Robinson), 28
Hospital chaplaincy, 41-42, 189-94
Hostility, in reconciling, 147
Hromádka, Josef, 123
Huckleberry Finn, 113
Hydraulic analogy of preaching, 60-61

Illinois Children's Hospital School, 192
Illustrations. *See* Cases
Images of ministry
administration, normative im-

Images of ministry—*cont'd*
age of, 76-80
author's view of, in evangelizing, 121-23, 126-27
as celebrating, 131-43
charismatic arms, 145, 146
church-as-mission, 114-16
clinical work, 109-10
common elements in, 209-11
custodian, 163
dialogic communication, 117-18
as disciplining, 173-83
doorbell ringing, 99-100, 110
as evangelizing, 112-30
as functional theologizing, 167-71
gavel-wielding, 146
handshaking, 145, 146
"higher" calling, 93-94
hired man, 160-61
"Holy Grail," 195
interview, 101-2, 111
itinerating, 161-62
meaning of, 16
medieval, 51-52, 56-58
mimeographing, 72-74
motherly teacher, 91-92
as passive theologizing, 163-67
pathologies of, in administering, 72-75; in preaching, 58-63
prayer, in disciplining, 173-75
as preaching, 51-68
as reconciling, 145-57
Reformation, 51-53
"repeat-after-me," 89-91
as revivalism, 112-13
as scholar, 162-63
as shepherding, 103-8

217

Personal self-discipline, 175-77
Pike, James A., 24
Police departments, chaplaincy to, 204
Power, in relation to ministry, 38, 44-45
Prayer, 173-75
Preaching, 51-68
  images of, 51-68
  relation of to pastoral care, 64-68
Preaching image
  analyzed, 53-63
  pathologies of, 58-63
Preface to Pastoral Theology (Hiltner), 9
Priests, 36, 37, 51, 52, 131, 132, 133
Princeton Theological Seminary, 9, 32, 153
Prison chaplaincy, 188-89
Professional, minister as, 46, 178-80
Professional self-discipline, 178-80
"Protestant confessional," 100-101
Psychology of administration, 81-84
Pulpit, in the preaching image of ministry, 53-56

Quakers, 38, 41, 156

Rabbinate, difference of from the ministry, 36
Reconciling, 144-57
  creating starting conditions for, 152-54
  in marriage counseling, 148-50

Reconciling—cont'd
  of nations, 153
  process of, 147-52
  in racial situations, 153
  in small groups, 147-48
  stages of, 147-52
  when it fails, 154-57
Reconciling image, 145-57
Reformation, the
  central image of ministry in, 51-53
  view of ministry in, 37-38
Reformed Pastor, The (Baxter), 87
Rehabilitation, chaplaincy in, 193
"Repeat-after-me" image, 89-91
Retirement, pastoral care in relation to, 198
Revivalist image, 112-14
Revolutionary groups, ministry to, 204-5
Risk in the ministry, 82
Ritual, 138-41
  function of, 139
  as like and unlike life, 139-40
  and obsessional neurosis, 149
  variety of responses to, 141
Robinson, John A. T., 24, 28
Rogers, Carl R., 102
Roman Catholic Church, 42, 51, 141
Roosevelt, Franklin D., 16
Rugged individualism in the ministry, 39
Rural centers, ministry to, 197

Sacrament, the, 131-36
Sacrament of the altar, 131-36
Sacrifice
  by Jesus Christ, 51, 57
  in Lord's Supper, 52-53, 133

220